MY REVISION NOTES

Pearson Edex

A-level

POLITICS: UK POLITICS

SECOND EDITION

Nick de Souza
Neil McNaughton

HODDER
EDUCATION
AN HACHETTE UK COMPANY

Orders: please contact Hachette UK Distribution, Hely Hutchinson Centre, Milton Road, Didcot, Oxfordshire, OX11 7HH. Telephone: +44 (0)1235 827827. Email education@hachette.co.uk. Lines are open from 9 a.m. to 5 p.m., Monday to Friday. You can also order through our website: www.hoddereducation.co.uk

© Nick de Souza and Neil McNaughton 2021

ISBN 978-1-3983-2553-1

First printed 2021

First published in 2021 by
Hodder Education,
An Hachette UK Company
Carmelite House
50 Victoria Embankment
London EC4Y 0DZ

www.hoddereducation.co.uk

Impression number   10 9 8 7 6 5 4 3

Year   2025 2024 2023 2022

Cover photo: nerthuz/Adobe Stock; other photos: p. 116 Tim Graham/Alamy Stock Photo; p. 117 David Gordon/Alamy Stock Photo; Süddeutsche Zeitung Photo/Alamy Stock Photo; p. 118 Zuma Press, Inc./Alamy Stock Photo

Typeset in India by Aptara, Inc.

Printed in Spain

A catalogue record for this title is available from the British Library.

MIX
Paper | Supporting
responsible forestry
FSC™ C104740

Get the most from this book

Everyone has to decide his or her own revision strategy, but it is essential to review your work, learn it and test your understanding. These Revision Notes will help you to do that in a planned way, topic by topic. Use this book as the cornerstone of your revision and do not hesitate to write in it — personalise your notes and check your progress by ticking off each section as you revise.

Tick to track your progress

Use the revision planner on pages 4–6 to plan your revision, topic by topic. Tick each box when you have:

+ revised and understood a topic
+ tested yourself
+ practised the exam questions and gone online to check your answers and complete the quick quizzes

You can also keep track of your revision by ticking off each topic heading in the book. You may find it helpful to add your own notes as you work through each topic.

Features to help you succeed

Exam tips

Expert tips are given throughout the book to help you polish your exam technique in order to maximise your chances in the exam.

Remember

The author provides advice to help you avoid common mistakes.

Now test yourself

These short, knowledge-based questions provide the first step in testing your learning. Answers are at **www.hoddereducation.co.uk/ myrevisionnotesdownloads**

Definitions and key words

Clear, concise definitions of essential key terms are provided where they first appear.

Key words from the specification are highlighted in blue throughout the book.

Making links

This feature identifies specific connections between topics and tells you how revising these will aid your exam answers.

Exam skills

These summaries highlight how specific skills identified or applicable in that chapter can be applied to your exam answers.

Revision activities

These activities will help you to understand each topic in an interactive way.

Exam practice

Practice exam questions are provided for each topic. Use them to consolidate your revision and practise your exam skills.

Summaries

The summaries provide a quick-check bullet list for each topic.

Online

Go online to check your answers to the exam questions and try out the extra quick quizzes at **www.hoddereducation.co.uk/ myrevisionnotesdownloads**

My Revision Notes: Pearson Edexcel A-Level Politics: UK politics second edition

My revision planner

REVISED   TESTED   EXAM READY

Answers and quick quizzes at **www.hoddereducation.co.uk/myrevisionnotesdownloads**

My Revision Notes: Pearson Edexcel A-Level Politics: UK politics second edition

Answers and quick quizzes at
www.hoddereducation.co.uk/myrevisionnotesdownloads

REVISED TESTED EXAM READY

Countdown to my exams

6–8 weeks to go

+ Start by looking at the specification — make sure you know exactly what material you need to revise and the style of the examination. Use the revision planner on pages 4–6 to familiarise yourself with the topics.
+ Organise your notes, making sure you have covered everything on the specification. The revision planner will help you to group your notes into topics.
+ Work out a realistic revision plan that will allow you time for relaxation. Set aside days and times for all the subjects that you need to study, and stick to your timetable.
+ Set yourself sensible targets. Break your revision down into focused sessions of around 40 minutes, divided by breaks. These Revision Notes organise the basic facts into short, memorable sections to make revising easier.

REVISED

4–6 weeks to go

+ Read through the relevant sections of this book and refer to the 'Remember' tips, key terms, Summaries and Exam skills boxes. Tick off the topics as you feel confident about them. Highlight those topics you find difficult and look at them again in detail.
+ Test your understanding of each topic by working through the 'Now test yourself' questions in the book. Check your answers online at **www.hoddereducation.co.uk/ myrevisionnotesdownloads**.
+ Make a note of any problem areas as you revise, and ask your teacher to go over these in class.
+ Look at past papers. They are one of the best ways to revise and practise your exam skills. Write or prepare planned answers to the exam practice questions provided in this book. Check your answers online and try out the extra quick quizzes.
+ Try using different revision methods as you work through the sections. For example, you can make notes using mind maps, spider diagrams or flash cards.
+ Track your progress using the revision planner and give yourself a reward when you have achieved your target.

REVISED

One week to go

+ Try to fit in at least one more timed practice of an entire past paper and seek feedback from your teacher, comparing your work closely with the mark scheme.
+ Check the revision planner to make sure you haven't missed out any topics. Brush up on any areas of difficulty by talking them over with a friend or getting help from your teacher.
+ Attend any revision classes put on by your teacher. Remember, your teacher is an expert at preparing people for examinations.

REVISED

The day before the examination

+ Flick through these Revision Notes for useful reminders, for example the 'Remember' tips, key terms, Summaries and Exam skills boxes.
+ Check the time and place of your examination.
+ Make sure you have everything you need — extra pens and pencils, tissues, a watch, bottled water, sweets.
+ Allow some time to relax and have an early night to ensure you are fresh and alert for the examination.

REVISED

My exams

Paper 1: UK Politics
Date:.................................
Time:.................................
Location:.................................

Paper 2: UK Government
Date:.................................
Time:.................................
Location:.................................

Paper 3: Comparative Politics
Date:.................................
Time:.................................
Location:.................................

Introduction

Key things to know about studying A-level Politics

This book covers the UK politics and UK government content of the course, which will come up in Papers 1 and 2. The ideologies and comparative content are covered in three other My Revision Notes books.

As a student of A-level Politics it is important that you know these six things about the examination:
+ the structure of the exam
+ the assessment objectives
+ the command word 'Evaluate' (and what this means)
+ the format of the source-based essay question
+ the synoptic element for Paper 2
+ the comparative sections in Paper 3

The structure of the exam

Paper 1: UK Politics (2 hours)
+ Answer **one** source-based essay question from a choice of two (30 marks).
+ Answer **one** non-source-based essay question from a choice of two (30 marks).
+ Answer **one** question on core ideologies from a choice of two (24 marks).

Total: 84 marks

Paper 2: UK Government (2 hours)
+ Answer **one** source-based essay question from a choice of two (30 marks).
+ Answer **one** non-source-based essay question from a choice of two (30 marks).
+ Answer **one** question on non-core ideologies from a choice of two (24 marks).

Total: 84 marks

Paper 3: Comparative Politics (2 hours)
+ Answer **one** comparative question from a choice of two (12 marks).
+ Answer **one** comparative theory question (12 marks).
+ Answer **two** essay questions from a choice of three (30 marks each).

Total: 84 marks

Types of question

In relation to the UK politics and UK government content covered in this book, there are two types of question that you will be asked:
+ the 30-mark source-based essay question in both Papers 1 and 2
+ the 30-mark non-source-based essay question in both Papers 1 and 2

Assessment objectives

Your answers will be marked by examiners who will look to see how well you have met the three assessment objectives. These are explained below:

Assessment objectives	Requirements
AO1: Knowledge and understanding	+ Identify/provide relevant arguments. + Provide relevant examples. + Use relevant and appropriate political terminology.
AO2: Analysis	+ Give a two-sided, balanced debate. + Develop and explain the arguments made.
AO3: Evaluation	+ Distinguish between strong and weak arguments. + Provide reasons for the judgements made.

What is meant by the word 'Evaluate'?

+ For the 30-mark source-based essay, the question will always start with the following words: 'Using the source, evaluate…'.
+ For the 30-mark non-source-based essay, the question will simply start with: 'Evaluate…'.

'Evaluate' means 'to judge' or 'to decide'. In the context of your exam, this usually means that you need to 'decide' whether something works, or if a proposal to change the political system would be beneficial.

The format of the source-based essay question

+ In the source-based question, the arguments that are used in your answer will need to come from the source that is provided. For an essay where there is not a source, arguments must come from your own knowledge.
+ The source is usually a short extract of just a few hundred words that contains content on both sides of a debate.

More guidance on answering these sorts of questions can be found at the end of Chapter 1.

The synoptic element for Paper 2

+ For the Paper 2 essay, you will need to refer to content — specifically key terms — from Paper 1.

More guidance on these synoptic links is provided at the end of Chapter 5.

The comparative sections in Paper 3

For Paper 3, you will follow either the Global Politics route or the Government and Politics of the USA route:
+ The USA route requires you to use your knowledge from UK Politics and UK Government to compare the two political systems.
+ The Global Politics route requires you to draw upon the core political theories that you learnt in the Core Political Ideas section of Paper 1.

These comparative sections will take the form of 12-mark questions (as outlined above). Guidance on how to answer these sections can be found in the other My Revision Notes books that cover A-level Politics.

What is democracy in general?

Before considering direct and representative democracy you should understand what the term 'democracy' means in its broadest sense. The following are commonly included criteria and can serve as a working definition when answering questions about democracy in general:

+ The people have **influence**, either direct or indirect, over political decisions.
+ Government and elected bodies or individuals are **accountable** to the people.
+ Government should operate within the **rule of law**, whereby all are equal under the law and government is subject to the same laws as the people.
+ **Elections** should be held regularly, they should be free and fair, and there should be universal adult suffrage.
+ These elections convey legitimacy upon the government.
+ **People should be free** to form political parties and other associations and to stand for elective office.
+ The **transition of power** from one government to the next must be peaceful.
+ The people should have access to **independent information** and opinion.
+ The **rights and freedoms** of the people should be respected by government.
+ Power should rest in **many places**, not just one.

> **Legitimacy** A situation whereby the outcome of elections is accepted, and the authority of government is recognised by the public.

Direct democracy

The characteristics of direct democracy are as follows:
+ The people make key decisions themselves.
+ Only in classical Greece has a whole system been described as direct democracy.
+ In its modern form, direct democracy uses initiatives and referendums. Other methods include public meetings and online consultations.
+ The UK is a representative democracy that uses direct democracy to resolve constitutional issues.

> **Direct democracy** A political system where the people themselves make political decisions. The modern equivalent is the use of referendums and initiatives within representative democracies.
>
> **Referendum** An occasion when voters are asked to decide upon an issue of public importance.

> **Remember**
>
> A direct democracy is a system where the people make all key decisions themselves, whereas a referendum is really only an example of a direct democratic method, sometimes used within representative democracies.

Representative democracy

The characteristics of representative democracy are as follows:
+ The people elect representatives to make political decisions on their behalf.
+ Regular elections are a key feature and the system is characterised by representative assemblies such as parliaments, assemblies and councils.
+ A government is elected to make key proposals and arrange for their implementation.
+ Government and elected representatives are accountable to the people.
+ Parties campaign to be able to represent the people in government.
+ Pressure groups operate, representing sections of society and various causes from outside the political system.

> **Representative democracy** A political system where the citizens elect representatives who make decisions on their behalf and are accountable to them.

> **Now test yourself**   TESTED ○
>
> 1 Describe three features of direct democracy.
> 2 Describe three features of representative democracy.
>
> **Answers online**

The similarities and differences between direct and representative democracy

Table 1.1 compares direct and representative democracy.

Table 1.1 Similarities and differences between direct and representative democracy

Similarities	Differences
Both systems involve voting and participation; only the nature of participation is different.	Voters do not elect an individual under direct democracy — they take part in referendums instead. Representative democracy involves voting for someone to represent voters' interests.
Some forms of direct democracy such as public meetings also require consultation, similar to representative democracy.	Voters consider a range of issues under representative democracy, whereas direct democracy often focuses on a specific issue.
Most forms of representative democracy involve some measure of direct democracy, and vice versa.	Voters in direct democracy are more actively involved in decision making whereas voters in representative democracy are more passive.

There are advantages and disadvantages of both direct and representative democracy, which are shown in Tables 1.2 and 1.3.

Table 1.2 The advantages and disadvantages of direct democracy

Advantage	Example	Disadvantage	Example/Explanation
Everyone gets a say in the decision.	The 2016 EU referendum was one of the greatest democratic exercises in British political history — more than 33 million people voted.	The decisions made by the people in referendums may be at odds with the preferences of their elected representatives, causing political instability.	The UK's political stability was severely compromised by the Brexit referendum.
Organisation is easier due to modern technology.	The growth of e-petitions has shown how easy it has become to find out what people think.	Impractical for large populations.	Emergency decisions often have to be made quickly and by only a handful of people.
Gives equal weight to all votes.	In a referendum, all votes are counted and the side with the most votes wins. In the EU referendum, 52% of voters opted to leave.	It can lead to the 'tyranny of the majority' (J. S. Mill).	A majority of voters in England voted for Brexit, while a majority in Scotland voted to remain. As the Leave side won, Scotland, as part of the UK, has left the EU.
Encourages popular participation.	Turnout for important referendums often exceeds general election turnout. The Scottish independence referendum in 2014 had 85% turnout, whereas the 2019 general election had just 67%.	Lack of accountability.	It is impossible to hold a whole voting population to account if a decision turns out to have unforeseen consequences.
Develops a sense of community and responsibility.	The Good Friday referendum in Northern Ireland paved the way for Catholics and Protestants to share power.	It can divide communities.	The EU referendum exposed and deepened divides between regions.
Encourages genuine debate.	The Electoral Reform Society found that the Scottish independence referendum was conducted in an open and honest way, with reasoned arguments.	It can allow an ill-educated populace to make ill-informed decisions.	The Electoral Reform Society found that many voters in the EU referendum felt confused about the information they received during the campaign.

Table 1.3 The advantages and disadvantages of representative democracy

Advantages	Example	Disadvantages	Example/Explanation
Accountability: the representative can be voted out.	Many Liberal Democrat MPs lost their seats in 2015 — the controversy over raising tuition fees resulted in the party losing the trust of its younger supporters.	Representatives do not always do what the people want and may just do what they want.	Liberal Democrat MPs had signed a pledge not to raise tuition fees after the 2010 general election but subsequently voted to do so.
Representatives can become experts.	Yvette Cooper MP is chair of the high-profile Home Affairs Select Committee, which focuses on immigration, crime and civil rights.	Political parties are dominated by individuals pursuing their own agendas.	After claiming that there was no 'magic money tree' for public services in the 2017 general election, Theresa May's Conservatives signed a deal with the Democratic Unionist Party, promising £1 billion of investment for Northern Ireland in return for that party's support in the House of Commons.
Practical for complex issues.	Addressing the Covid-19 pandemic required MPs to weigh up the difficulties faced by small businesses during lockdown alongside the scientific necessity to minimise social contact.	Politicians can be incompetent or corrupt.	Former cabinet minister Chris Huhne MP was found guilty of perverting the course of justice, and so too was former Labour MP Fiona Onasanya.
Gives a voice to minority opinion.	Parliament has passed several laws extending the rights of citizens, including the Human Rights Act and Freedom of Information Act.	Minority groups might still find that their concerns are unmet.	MPs voted down proposed amendments to the bill authorising withdrawal from the EU in 2020 that would have protected child refugees.
Trains future leaders of the country.	Boris Johnson held prominent roles in the cabinets of both prime ministers David Cameron and Theresa May before becoming prime minister himself in 2019.	Not all voters get the representative they want.	The first-past-the-post electoral system has meant that smaller parties are under-represented in Parliament.

Pluralism and democracy

The term 'pluralism' or 'pluralist democracy' implies the following aspects of a society and a political system:

+ Power and influence are widely dispersed among the people and among sections of society — power is not excessively concentrated in a few hands.
+ There is acceptance, both legal and cultural, of a wide range of minorities, political beliefs, religions, types of people and cultures.
+ Political parties are free to operate and campaign and there are many parties which citizens may choose to support.
+ Pressure groups and campaign groups are tolerated and allowed to operate freely.
+ There is a range of sources of independent information, news and opinion available to the people without interference by the state.

> **Pluralist democracy**
> A political system and/ or society where there is widespread acceptance of different groups and lifestyles, where freedom of expression and association are respected, where many parties and pressure groups may operate and where there are independent media. The term also implies that power is dispersed and not concentrated.

An overall assessment of democracy in the UK

Table 1.4 offers an assessment of UK democracy. The 'problem/barriers' column summarises the democratic deficit in the UK as described by many critics.

> **Democratic deficit** Where standards of a functioning democracy have fallen short.

Table 1.4 An assessment of UK democracy

Feature	How this feature works in practice in the UK	Problem/barriers preventing this feature from working effectively
Pluralism: power lies in many different places (judges, Parliament, prime minister etc.).	+ The 2017 Article 50 decision on Britain leaving the EU involved a number of institutions, not just the prime minister. Parliament voted on it, judges ruled on it and the people expressed their opinion in a referendum.	+ Others argue that power is instead concentrated in the hands of a few people and organisations. + The Institute of Economic Affairs (IEA) has been accused of using cash to gain influence over ministers.
Free and fair elections	+ All adults can vote, and the results are trusted and accepted.	+ 16- and 17-year-olds and prisoners cannot vote in general elections. + The first-past-the-post electoral system is unfair and leads to 'elected dictatorship' (Lord Hailsham).
Corruption and wrongdoing are punished.	+ In 2019 two MPs, Fiona Onasanya and Chris Davies, were successfully recalled (see section on the recall of MPs on p. 83).	+ There is a perception of corruption among some representatives (cash for peerages affair and the MPs' expenses scandal). + In 2020 Boris Johnson failed to explain the £15,000 holiday he received from Carphone Warehouse tycoon David Ross.
Citizens' rights are protected.	+ The Human Rights Act allows citizens to use UK courts to protect their rights under the European Convention on Human Rights (ECHR).	+ The Human Rights Act is not entrenched (see Chapter 5), which means that it could be scrapped with an act of parliament.
Devolved decision making	+ Devolution has resulted in the transfer of power from central government to regional and local bodies, such as the Scottish and Welsh Parliaments.	+ Devolution is still limited. + Some 85% of local council budgets in England still comes from central government.

The franchise

The franchise refers to the 'right to vote'. It has been fought for over many centuries but the UK currently enjoys 'universal adult suffrage'. The principles of UK suffrage are as follows:
+ Everyone over the age of 18 has the right to vote in elections, save for a limited few such as convicted prisoners, people who are certified as insane and members of the royal family.
+ No groups are discriminated against in electoral law.
+ It is the responsibility of each individual to register to vote.

Franchise or suffrage Both terms essentially mean the right to vote. In modern democracies suffrage is extended to all adults, with no groups excluded. A system which does exclude some or all citizens from voting cannot be described as democratic.

Political participation

The following are forms of political participation:
+ voting in elections
+ joining a political party
+ becoming an *active* member of a party
+ joining a trade union
+ standing for election to office
+ joining a pressure group
+ becoming *active* in a pressure group
+ taking part in a political campaign online or on the ground
+ signing a petition or e-petition

Possible reasons why turnout at elections is falling include the following:
+ disillusionment with political parties, especially among younger people, and a falling commitment to parties (partisan dealignment)
+ people being more concerned with single issues than with broad policies
+ a lack of distinction between the parties since the 1990s
+ the electoral system results in large numbers of wasted votes (for smaller parties and in safe seats) and votes of unequal value (marginal versus safe seats), and also results in disproportional outcomes for third parties
+ with the emergence of referendums, voters prefer direct democracy

A participation crisis?

Table 1.5 considers whether there is a participation crisis in the UK.

Table 1.5 Is there a participation crisis in the UK?

> **Participation crisis** A concern that fewer people are taking part in political activity, leading to a crisis in democratic legitimacy.

Form of participation	There is a crisis	There is not a crisis
Voting in general elections	+ 67.3% turnout in the 2019 general election — down 1.5% from the 2017 one. + This figure is well below the high levels of the 1970s, where turnout reached 78.8% in 1974.	+ From 2001 to 2017, general election turnout steadily increased. + There could be several reasons why the turnout fell in 2019, including the time of year (December) in which the election was held.
Joining a political party	+ Only around 1.7% of the population are members of a political party.	+ Labour Party membership rose considerably after 2015 when Jeremy Corbyn became leader.
Union membership	+ The number of private-sector employees belonging to a trade union constitutes only 13% of the private-sector workforce.	+ Overall union membership has risen for four consecutive years to 2020.
Signing petitions	+ It is difficult to claim that taking 3 minutes to sign a petition amounts to meaningful participation.	+ 38 Degrees claims that almost 40 million people have signed an e-petition on its website, concerning over 10,000 campaigns.
Joining a pressure group	+ Many 'cheque-book' members pay membership fees and do little else.	+ Fair Funding for Schools engaged teachers, headteachers and parents in campaigning against education cuts.

Exam tip

Examiners like you to come to a clear decision, so try to avoid arguing that there is a participation crisis 'to an extent'. What is even better is to take a clear decision about specific forms of participation. For example, you could write, 'There is clearly a participation crisis when considering party membership but not in other non-traditional forms of participation such as e-petition use.'

Now test yourself

6 Give one argument, and an example, to show that there is a participation crisis when it comes to voting.

7 Give one argument, and an example, to show that there is not a participation crisis when it comes to voting.

Answers online

1 Democracy and participation

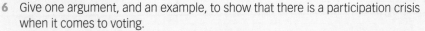

How to improve political participation in the UK

Different suggestions have been made on how to improve political participation in the UK. These include lowering the voting age, making voting compulsory and utilising online forms of political activity. There has also been a debate about convenience voting.

Table 1.6 considers different ways of improving participation.

Table 1.6 Suggested methods to improve political participation in the UK

Method to improve participation	Arguments for	Arguments against
Lowering the voting age for general elections	+ 16- and 17-year-olds in Scotland and Wales can already vote in local and regional elections. + Youth turnout in the Scottish independence referendum reached 80%.	+ Many young people do not vote — only 43% of 18–24-year-olds voted in the 2015 general election.
Compulsory voting	+ Turnout would reach 100%. + Other countries have compulsory voting, such as Australia.	+ Voting is a right, not a duty. + People may spoil their ballot papers.
Voting online	+ Online voting has proven successful in Estonia. + It may boost youth turnout.	+ It is subject to breaches in cybersecurity. + For most people, voting in person is already easy enough.

Convenience voting refers to any measure that makes it easier to vote, including postal voting, online voting, voting on the weekend, voting anywhere in the constituency rather than at a specific polling booth (e.g. at supermarket polling stations and places of work) and voting over multiple days.

Exam tip

When answering questions about ways in which the participation crisis might be solved or how democracy in the UK might be improved, it is important that you do not merely describe the changes proposed but also explain *why* they might work. For example, why might the introduction of proportional representation improve election turnout?

Now test yourself

8 Outline three ways in which voting could be made more 'convenient'.

9 Complete the table below on lowering the voting age.

Arguments in favour of lowering the voting age	Arguments against lowering the voting age
1	1
2	2

Answers online

The nature of pressure groups

A pressure group is an organisation that seeks to influence public policy. There are two main types of pressure groups, promotional and sectional.

Promotional groups

+ They are altruistic in that they serve the whole community, not just their own members and supporters.
+ They tend to concentrate on mobilising public opinion and putting pressure on government in that way. They seek widespread support.
+ They often use 'direct action' in the form of public demonstrations, internet campaigns and sometimes civil disobedience.
+ They often, but not always, focus on one specific issue or a range of issues relating to a general cause.
+ Example: Black Lives Matter focuses strongly on police treatment of people from minority ethnic groups

Sectional groups

+ They are largely (although not always) self-interested in that they serve the interests of their own members and supporters.
+ Although they seek public support, they tend to promote direct links with decision makers (achieving insider status).
+ Their methods tend to be more subtle and less in the public eye, and they often take the parliamentary route to influence.
+ They usually have a formal, closed membership.
+ Often, sectional groups represent a specific section of the workforce.
+ Example: the National Education Union primarily looks after the interests of teachers.

Differences between pressure groups and political parties

The differences between pressure groups and political parties are explored in Table 1.7 below.

Table 1.7 Nature of parties and pressure groups

Area of comparison	Parties	Pressure groups
Power	Seek to gain power or a share of power	Do not generally seek governmental power
Accountability	Have to make themselves accountable to the electorate	Not accountable except to their own members
Policies	Develop policies across all or most areas of government responsibility	Usually have narrower concerns and sometimes are concerned with only one issue
Membership	Usually have a formal membership and some kind of formal organisation	Often have supporters rather than members

> **Remember**
>
> While there are clear differences between most pressure groups and political parties, some pressure groups transform themselves into political parties in order to stand candidates for elections and bring more attention to a particular cause. The National Health Action Party stood candidates for a number of elections to raise awareness of NHS cuts.

Pressure group methods

Table 1.8 shows a list of pressure group methods along with examples of groups that typically use such methods. Pressure groups use different methods for different purposes, and these methods change as society and technology evolve.

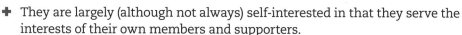

17

Table 1.8 Pressure group methods

Method	Description and example
Lobbying	This involves persuasion through direct contact with important decision makers, policy makers and legislators. Sometimes professional lobby organisations may be used. It is used largely by **insider groups**, such as the National Farmers' Union (NFU), British Bankers' Association (BBA) and Confederation of British Industry (CBI). 'Mass lobbying' of Parliament is also used. Example: Age UK lobbies MPs on behalf of pensioners.
Public campaigning	This involves large-scale demonstrations of support for an issue or a group. It is designed to mobilise public opinion and to show the level of support to decision makers. Examples: pro-remain demonstrations (organised by People's Vote) and pro-leave demonstrations following the EU referendum.
Donations to political parties	These are legal as long as they are declared. They are typically used by large corporations and employer organisations or by trade unions. Example: Open Democracy found that the Conservative Party received £11 million from property developers in Boris Johnson's first year as prime minister.
Media campaigns	These often feature celebrities and mobilise public support. Examples: the 2020 campaign to continue free school meals over the summer holidays (Marcus Rashford) and efforts to reduce the stigma for those suffering from poor mental health (Princes William and Harry).
Civil disobedience	When other methods have failed, illegal methods may be used. Examples: Extinction Rebellion (blocking roads and bridges), Plane Stupid (opposing airport expansion by invading runways). The suffragettes also engaged in civil disobedience, which ranged from women chaining themselves to railings at Buckingham Palace to defacing valuable works of art.
Social media and e-petitions	Social media can be used to raise awareness and gain support, and to organise e-petitions and local action. Examples: the successful campaign to scrap the tampon tax resulted in the government agreeing to scrap VAT on sanitary products from 2021. The e-petition to accept more Syrian refugees in 2015 received 460,000 signatures.
Legal action	Judicial reviews aim to prevent discrimination against women and minorities and to preserve much-needed public services. Examples: the Save Lewisham Hospital Campaign won a legal battle in 2013 when the Court of Appeal ruled that the government did not have the legal authority to close Lewisham Hospital. The civil liberties organisation Liberty won a case against police use of facial recognition technology in August 2020.

Insider groups Pressure groups with access to decision makers, which means that their tactics tend to be more discreet and behind closed doors, relying upon a network of close links to advisors and politicians. Outsider groups do not usually have such close contact with decision makers and therefore need to resort to methods that seek public support and media attention.

Remember

It is important to use recent examples when writing about pressure groups. It is particularly useful to use a case study, referring back to it in different sections of your essay. For example, you can refer to how Extinction Rebellion took part in civil disobedience by blocking roads and also refer to how it has used social media.

Now test yourself   TESTED ⬤

10 Complete the table below by providing examples for each pressure group method.

Method	Example
Civil disobedience	
Use of celebrities	
Donations to political parties	

11 Describe two differences between outsider and insider pressure groups.

Answers online

Pressure group influence

Table 1.9 reviews the factors that affect pressure group success.

Table 1.9 Factors that affect pressure group success

Factor	How this factor increases the likelihood of pressure group success and influence	How this factor might not guarantee pressure group success and influence
Insider status	Insider groups may be given the opportunity to offer their views on draft legislation. Example: private healthcare companies helped draft the controversial Health and Social Care bill that they themselves stood to benefit from.	Not all insider groups are influential in every circumstance. Example: the Confederation of British Industry (CBI) has strong ties to the Conservative Party but has not been able to influence government policy on Brexit in the way it would like to.
Group size	A larger membership can be important in persuading government that a pressure group reflects a significant section of public opinion. Example: The Campaign to Protect Rural England has 40,000 members and has been largely successful in defending the green belt from property development.	Larger group size does not always bring success. Example: the Campaign for Nuclear Disarmament had an estimated 110,000 members in the mid-1980s but arguably had little influence on government.
Public support	Pressure groups that can demonstrate large-scale public support are more likely to have influence. Example: the Snowdrop Campaign to ban the use of handguns was successful largely because of the public reaction to the 1996 Dunblane primary school massacre.	Government attitudes may matter more than public opinion. Example: the 2013 badger cull went ahead, regardless of the public outcry and concern from animal welfare groups.

> **Exam tip**
>
> When it comes to pressure groups, be prepared for an exam question that asks you whether one factor is the most important factor that affects pressure group influence. For example:
>
> *Evaluate the view that public support is the most important factor that determines the success of pressure groups in influencing politicians.*
>
> The words 'most important' invite you to consider the factor in the question and compare its importance with other factors (such as the status of the pressure group etc.). You will need to take a clear direction — public support either *is* the most important factor or it *isn't*.

Pressure groups and democracy

You should be able to consider the question of whether pressure groups threaten democracy or enhance it. This is explored in Table 1.10.

Table 1.10 Do pressure groups enhance or threaten democracy?

Pressure groups enhance democracy	Pressure groups may threaten democracy
They help to disperse power and influence more widely. Example: the British Medical Association (BMA) ensures that the voice of the medical community is heard when it comes to health policy.	Some groups are elitist and tend to concentrate power in the hands of too few people. Example: the 'revolving door' involves special advisors to ministers getting well-paid jobs at lobbying firms, where they can exploit the contacts they made while in government.
They educate the public about important political issues. Example: the Act for the Act campaign, founded in 2015, raised awareness of how the Human Rights Act has helped ordinary people.	Some groups may distort information or seek to limit social and technological progress. Example: Stop 5G is a group that is concerned about the potential health and environmental effects of 5G, but its claims are hotly contested. Some argue that instead of focusing on the negative effects of 5G, which are yet to be proven, it is better to focus on the economic benefits that 5G rollout could bring.

My Revision Notes: Pearson Edexcel A-Level Politics: UK politics second edition

Pressure groups enhance democracy	Pressure groups may threaten democracy
They give people more opportunities to participate in politics without having to sacrifice too much of their time and attention. Example: while more than 16 million registered voters chose not to cast their ballot at the 2019 general election, 38 Degrees estimates that nearly 40 million people have signed an e-petition since 2013.	Those that are internally undemocratic may not accurately represent the views of their members and supporters. Example: many pressure group leaders are unelected.
They can promote and protect the interests and rights of minorities. Example: the Howard League fights for better prison conditions for prison inmates. They help to call government to account by publicising the effects of policy. Example: Justice4Grenfell pushed for a public inquiry into the Grenfell Tower fire.	Finance is a key factor in political influence so groups that are wealthy may wield a disproportionate amount of influence. Example: in 2020, housing minister Robert Jenrick was accused of rushing through approval of a development project to satisfy Tory donor Richard Desmond, a property developer.

Now test yourself

TESTED ◯

12 Why might a pressure group be able to exert influence? Next to each factor, write an explanation.

Factor	Explanation
Insider status	
Group size	
Public support	

13 Outline three arguments that pressure groups enhance democracy.

Answers online

Think tanks, lobbyists and corporations

Think tanks

REVISED ◯

There are various examples of think tanks which may influence policy. Many of them can be said to have either a left-wing or right-wing bias, which can affect which political party they influence.
+ Non-partisan think tanks include ResPublica, which focuses on general policy issues, and Chatham House, which prioritises international affairs.
+ 'Left-wing' think tanks include the Fabian Society, dealing with issues mainly concerning social justice and equality, and the Institute for Public Policy Research (IPPR), which researches and develops various centre-left policy ideas.
+ 'Right-wing' think tanks include the Adam Smith Institute, which researches and develops free market solutions to economic issues, and the Centre for Policy Studies, which promotes the ideas popular in the premiership of Margaret Thatcher.

> **Think tank** A body of experts brought together to investigate and offer solutions to economic, social and political problems.

Lobbyists

REVISED ◯

Lobbyists are professionals who are paid to persuade decision makers to favour a particular group or cause. They might be individuals or companies and are often employed by businesses, employer groups, pressure groups (e.g. Animal Aid), professional associations, trade unions and even foreign governments.

> **Lobbyists** Individuals or companies paid to persuade decision makers to favour a particular group or cause.

Corporations

A corporation is a large company or a group of companies that operate as a single entity. Corporations' wealth is often so great, and their importance to the UK economy so large, that governments cannot easily ignore them.

Impact on politics

Table 1.11 analyses the impact of think tanks, lobbyists and corporations on UK politics.

Table 1.11 Impact of think tanks, lobbyists and corporations on UK politics

Group	Influence	Limits to influence
Think tanks	The Centre for Social Justice had an enormous impact on the 2010–15 coalition government welfare reforms that resulted in the introduction of universal credit.	Think tanks aligned to a political party (e.g. the left-leaning IPPR) lose influence when that party is not in power.
Lobbyists	Lobbying firms spend around £2 billion each year seeking to influence decision makers. They employ around 4,000 people. Concerns have been raised that influence can be bought.	Regulations ban MPs from accepting money from lobbyists in return for agreeing to represent lobbyists' viewpoints.
Corporations	Corporations donate to political party election campaigns and they also fund think tanks. Over a fifth of Conservative Party donations came from corporations in the run-up to the 2019 general election.	Corporations do not always get the policies they want. For example, most large corporations opposed Brexit.

> **Exam tip**
>
> Make sure you write about what the question asks. If you are asked about think tanks and lobbyists, you should only write about them and not corporations or other pressure groups. Keep repeating the words in the question in every paragraph to help keep your writing relevant. It might help to use this sentence starter in each paragraph: 'This point is relevant to the question because...'.

Now test yourself

14 Identify an example of a particular pressure group that might carry out the function or use the methods described in the table below.

Description	Example
An organisation that seeks to mobilise public opinion through the use of mass demonstrations	
An organisation that operates on behalf of business and seeks to influence ministers and parliamentarians directly	
An organisation that tends to use illegal methods or civil disobedience to gain public attention	
An organisation that has local concerns and typically uses social media to organise protest	
An organisation that uses insider status to represent the interests of a particular section of society	

15 Identify the differences between pressure groups and political parties.

Answers online

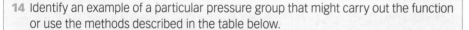

1 Democracy and participation

21

The development of rights in the UK

What are the sources of rights in the UK? The following examples show where our rights have come from:

✚ **Magna Carta.** This document, issued in 1215, was the first document that set out the limits of the king's power. It sought to prevent the government from exploiting its power. While it initially sought to protect barons against an all-powerful king, the Magna Carta has now come to symbolise the right of the people to be free from a government acting beyond the power given to it in law.

✚ **Common law.** This has developed over many centuries. These are rights which have been recognised as existing and commonly enforced. They are confirmed by judicial precedent — judgments made in the courts and enforced by lower courts. Examples: the rule of law guaranteeing equal treatment under the law, habeas corpus (freedom from imprisonment without trial), rules relating to a fair trial.

✚ **Statutes.** Parliamentary law may guarantee rights. Example: the Freedom of Information Act 2000 (granting the right to access official information).

✚ **The Human Rights Act.** This law brought the European Convention on Human Rights into UK law. A wide range of rights and freedoms are guaranteed.

✚ **Equalities Act 2010.** This law legally protects people against discrimination in the workplace and in wider society, specifically on the basis of age, disability, gender reassignment, marital status, race, religion, sex and sexual orientation.

> **Remember**
>
> Many students mistakenly believe that the European Convention on Human Rights (ECHR) is controlled by the European Union. This would imply that now the UK has left the EU, all these rights are lost. This is not so. The ECHR is administered by a different body, the Council of Europe, and its European Court of Human Rights. It has nothing to do with the EU and therefore the rights in the ECHR continue to apply to UK citizens, regardless of Brexit.

How well are rights protected in the UK?

Table 1.12 outlines the strengths and weaknesses of rights protection in the UK.

Table 1.12 An assessment of rights protection in the UK

Strengths	Weaknesses
There is a strong common law tradition. Examples: the rights of cohabiting couples; the right to a fair trial.	Common law can be vague and disputed. It can also be set aside by parliamentary statutes. Example: the government introduced internment in Northern Ireland (imprisonment without trial of suspected terrorists) in the 1970s.
The UK is subject to the European Convention on Human Rights (ECHR). Example: the European Court of Human Rights ruled that prisoners in the UK have the right to vote.	Parliament remains sovereign and so can ignore the ECHR or can even repeal the Human Rights Act. Example: prisoners have not yet been given the right to vote in the UK, despite the European Court of Human Rights' ruling.
The judiciary has a reputation for being independent and upholding the rule of law even against the expressed wishes of government and Parliament. Example: in April 2016, judges overturned government plans to deny legal aid to people who have not lived in the UK continuously for at least 12 months.	There is increasing pressure on government, as a result of international terrorism, to curtail rights in the interests of national security. The right to privacy, the right of association and expression as well as freedom from imprisonment without trial are all threatened. Example: in 2016, the Conservative government passed the Investigatory Powers Act ('snoopers' charter').

Now test yourself

TESTED ⬤

16 Outline three ways in which rights are protected in the UK.

Answers online

Conflicts between individual and collective rights

There are constant conflicts between the principle of individual rights and the collective rights of the community as a whole — see Table 1.13.

Table 1.13 Conflicts between individuals' rights and collective rights

Individual rights	Conflicting collective rights
Freedom of expression	The rights of minority groups not to be subjected to hate speech
The right to privacy	The right of the community to be protected from terrorism by security services which may listen in on private communications
The individual right to privacy	The collective right of the press to report on matters of public interest
The right to demonstrate in public places (right of association and free movement)	The right of the community to their own freedom of movement
The right to strike in pursuit of pay and employment rights	The right of the community to expect good service from public servants who are paid from taxation

Individual rights Rights that belong to a person regardless of personal characteristics. They apply to all individuals regardless of race, religion or gender.

Collective rights Rights that belong to a group. This group might share a particular characteristic (e.g. gay rights) or it might be a group in an organisation (e.g. workers' rights).

Case study: the Ashers bakery case

In October 2018, the UK Supreme Court ruled that a baker could not be compelled to write 'Support gay marriage' on a cake, which was requested by a customer for a same-sex wedding. The decision appears to have upheld the individual right of a baker to their freedom of conscience — they could not be compelled to write something that went against their own beliefs. However, in coming to this decision, the court may have affected the collective right of the LGBTQ+ community to equal access to services (in this instance buying a cake of their choice).

Exam tip

When answering a question on whether rights are protected in the UK, it is important to acknowledge that individual rights might sometimes be in conflict with collective rights, as the 'Ashers bakery case' shows.

Now test yourself

TESTED ⬤

17 Identify the specific development that matches each purpose in relation to rights in the table below.

Purpose	Development (with date if applicable)
A piece of legislation guaranteeing a wide range of rights and liberties	
A piece of legislation giving citizens access to official documents and information	
A historical phenomenon stretching back centuries that guarantees anciently held rights	
A piece of legislation outlawing discrimination against women and minorities	

18 Describe three sources of rights in the UK.

Answers online

23

Pressure groups and rights

There are a number of pressure groups concerned with rights in the UK. Table 1.14 details these groups and indicates the limits to their success.

Table 1.14 Pressure groups concerned with rights

Rights group	Description/focus	Limits to success
Liberty	Probably the best-known group, it is a major campaigner and think tank that primarily focuses on limiting government power and protecting citizens' rights.	The group has frequently opposed government proposals for mass surveillance after terror attacks, which has not always proven popular.
Unlock Democracy	This group is concerned with many constitutional reform issues, among which are methods of strengthening rights protection, including a codified constitution containing a bill of rights.	Constitutional issues are not high up on the agenda of either of the two major political parties.
Amnesty International	Investigates and campaigns against human rights abuses around the world. In the UK, it has been involved in numerous campaigns, including over the rights of those in care homes during the Covid-19 lockdowns, defending victims of the Windrush scandal and campaigning for the legalisation of abortion in Northern Ireland.	Amnesty International is often dependent on governments being willing to admit they were wrong and to change their policies. For example, very few victims of the Windrush scandal have been paid compensation.
The Fawcett Society	Campaigns for gender equality and women's rights at work, specifically reducing the gender pay gap and increasing female representation in politics. Much of the group's work focuses on research and lobbying.	There is public frustration at the slow pace of reform, perhaps leading many women to look to the #MeToo campaign and to public protest instead.
JUSTICE	Largely made up of members of the legal profession, campaigning for rights protection, especially in the area of law enforcement and trials.	The war on terror and fight against extremism have meant that the law surrounding the rights and trials of suspects has moved in favour of the prosecution, particularly with the introduction of closed material procedures (the ability of the state to produce evidence that the defence is not allowed to see).

Exam tip

When you are discussing rights, the examiners will wish to see examples of how rights campaign groups are seeking to improve rights protection. It is worthwhile, therefore, to give some examples of the work of the rights groups identified in this section.

Exam practice

1 Evaluate the view that the UK remains a genuine pluralist democracy. [30]

2 Evaluate the view that rights are effectively protected in the UK. [30]

3 Using the source, evaluate the view that representative democracy is superior to direct democracy. [30]

It is natural to assume that direct democracy is the purest form of political system that can exist. After all, it represents the ultimate form of government by consent and, at the same time, it means that the majority rules. It is also to be expected that the people are more likely to respect decisions they have made themselves.

Direct democracy does, however, have some illustrious critics. In classical Greece, the philosopher Plato argued that it would give rise to the rule of rabble-rousing dictators who would be able to sway opinion through great speeches and appeals to popular emotion. Today we see echoes of this in the way the tabloid press often treats referendum campaigns. In nineteenth-century England, the great liberal thinker John Stuart Mill referred to the 'tyranny of the majority' and, like Plato, feared that the average citizen, lacking much education, would not act rationally and would be ignorant of the issues presented to them. Mill and his fellow nineteenth-century liberals supported representative democracy. This was for several reasons.

First, they argued that elected representatives would be able to use their superior judgement in the interests of the people and would be able to arbitrate between the interests of the majority and those of minorities. Second, they believed that this compromise would satisfy the liberal desire to ensure that all sections of society are considered in political decision making. Third, they had little faith in the people's ability to reach rational decisions.

It is hardly surprising, therefore, that representative democracy has now become the norm in modern liberal-based political systems. Nevertheless, there are now signs that direct democracy is creeping back into fashion. In the UK, considered to be the original cradle of representative democracy, governments are increasingly resorting to referendums, the modern form of direct democracy. Referendums are often used to settle constitutional issues and occasions when government itself is unable to resolve an issue without excessive conflict.

Source: original material

In your response you must:
+ compare and contrast the different opinions in the source
+ examine and debate these views in a balanced way
+ analyse and evaluate only the information presented in the source

Answers and quick quiz 1 online

Exam skills

Below is a sample paragraph that uses the content of Table 1.10 to answer the following question:

Evaluate the view that pressure groups threaten rather than enhance democracy. (30 marks)

The student takes the view that pressure groups do not threaten democracy.

There are those who incorrectly argue that pressure groups are elitist and tend to concentrate power in the hands of too few people. They might point to the so-called 'revolving door', which involves special advisors to ministers getting well-paid jobs at lobbying firms, where they can exploit the contacts they made while in government. This point is relevant to the question as it suggests that too few people have a say in decision making, which thus threatens democracy. However, supporters of this view fail to point out that pressure groups help to disperse power and influence more widely. For example, the BMA ensures that the voice of the medical community is heard when it comes to health policy. If thousands of pressure groups help those whose voices would otherwise not be heard, then it is clear that pressure groups enhance rather than threaten democracy.

This paragraph does a number of things really well:
+ It is two-sided, which helps the student show good analysis (AO2).
+ It explains the arguments (also helping with AO2), using sentence starters that signpost when doing so ('This point is relevant to the question…').
+ The paragraph uses two relevant examples, helping the student to gain marks for displaying their knowledge (AO1).
+ The student takes a clear direction, signposting the arguments they agree and disagree with ('There are those who incorrectly argue…'). This approach helps the student demonstrate good evaluation skills (AO3). →

For source-based questions it is important to remember the tips contained in the table below.

Source-based essay tip	How this tip can be applied to Exam practice question 3 above
Read the question and decide whether you agree/disagree.	Decide whether you think that representative democracy or direct democracy is better.
Using two different-coloured highlighters, identify arguments that you agree with and disagree with.	Best to use green for the arguments you agree with and red for the arguments you don't agree with.
Devise a plan that shows which two competing source arguments you will develop in each paragraph. Make sure the argument and counter-argument have some kind of link or common theme.	You could contrast the argument that direct democracy 'means that the majority rules' with the fear expressed by John Stuart Mill regarding the 'tyranny of the majority'.
All arguments should come from the source.	While it is perfectly fine to use your own examples to expand upon the arguments in the source, you will not be credited for bringing in arguments that are not in the source. The source above does not mention how technology has made it easier to consult directly with the people, so you should not use this point.

Summary

You should now have an understanding of:

+ the distinction between direct and representative democracy
+ the state of democracy in the UK — you will need at least three negative features and at least three positive features
+ proposals to improve participation and the strengths and weaknesses of these proposals
+ pressure groups — it is essential that you have contemporary examples to illustrate your analysis of their activities and the extent to which they have been successful
+ the ways in which external groups seek to influence government and other decision makers — including examples of not only pressure groups but also think tanks, large corporations and lobbyists
+ the debate around whether pressure groups enhance or threaten democracy
+ the status of rights in the UK — you will need plenty of examples of which rights are enforced and which are endangered

2 Political parties

Features of political parties

+ Parties are associations of people who hold similar political views and wish to promote those views.
+ Parties seek to gain governmental power at local, regional and national levels. The search for power distinguishes parties from other associations.
+ Most parties have some kind of formal organisation, normally a hierarchy including leaders, activists and followers.
+ Most parties have a system of membership.

Functions of political parties

The main functions of political parties are to:
+ improve society
+ select suitable candidates for office at all levels — local, regional and national
+ identify and train political leaders, again at local, regional and national levels
+ educate the public about important political issues
+ provide organised opportunities for people to participate in politics
+ when not in government, call the existing government to account

Parties are an integral part of the UK political system — they help to organise elections and to run the business of representative bodies at local, regional and national levels.

> **Remember**
>
> Do not confuse 'functions' with 'features'. Functions refers to what a body or association such as a party does, what its purposes are. Features refers to what it looks like, its main characteristics.

The funding of political parties

Political parties have a number of different sources of finance, including:
+ membership subscriptions
+ fundraising events such as fetes, festivals, conferences and dinners
+ donations from supporters
+ loans from wealthy individuals or banks
+ self-financing of candidates for office

There is up to £2 million per party available in grants from the Electoral Commission, plus Short money, which grants funds to parties for research, depending on their size.

The proposals for reform of party funding include the following:
+ Impose restrictions on the size of individual donations to parties. This is broadly the system used in the USA (though donors can grant funds to thousands of individual candidates). To be effective the cap would have to be relatively low.
+ Impose tight restrictions on how much parties are allowed to spend. This would make large-scale fundraising futile.
+ Restrict donations to individuals.
+ Replace all funding with state grants for parties, paid for out of general taxation.

27

State funding is the most prominent and controversial proposal for reform. Table 2.1 shows the arguments in favour of and against the state funding of parties.

Table 2.1 The debate about state funding of parties

Arguments for	Arguments against
It will end the opportunities for the corrupt use of donations (often known as 'cash for honours'). Some donors give money in the expectation of being granted an honour or access to decision makers. Example: Tory donor Lubov Chernukhin, whose husband was closely associated with Vladimir Putin, paid £1.7 million to the Conservative Party and has enjoyed personal meetings with the last three Conservative prime ministers.	Taxpayers may object to funding what can be considered to be 'private' organisations. There are many other calls on government revenue which are seen as more important.
It will end the possibility of 'hidden' forms of influence through funding. Organisations and companies often deny they are seeking political advantage, but this claim is difficult to justify. Example: the £1 million donation from Formula 1 boss Bernie Ecclestone before the 1997 election appeared to influence the Labour government policy on banning tobacco advertising, once it had won office, as Labour initially exempted this sport from the ban.	It will be difficult to know how to distribute funding. Should it be on the basis of past performance (in which case large parties will retain their advantage) or on the basis of future aspirations (which is vague)? Example: The 2007 Phillips Report recommended a 'pence-per-voter' formula for greater state funding of parties. Yet this formula would serve only to benefit the two main parties that receive the most votes.
It could reduce the huge financial advantage that large parties enjoy and give smaller parties the opportunity to make progress. In the run-up to general elections, smaller parties often have to rely on taking out loans that can put their long-term viability in jeopardy.	Parties may lose some of their independence and will see themselves as organs of the state.
It will improve democracy by ensuring wider participation from groups that have no ready source of funds.	It may lead to excessive state regulation of parties. Example: the Political Parties, Elections and Referendums Act (PPERA) 2000 already imposes overall limits on party spending in general elections and in other elections, to make parties less reliant on wealthy individual backers. Any further regulation may limit their ability to campaign effectively.

Exam tip

Make sure you consider in advance how to approach questions that require you to 'evaluate' a view. If the question is 'Evaluate the view that parties should receive state funding', you should already know which side you are on. If you believe that parties should receive state funding, your introduction should end with a sentence like this one: 'The direction of this essay is that parties should receive state funding.'

Now test yourself   TESTED

1 Give two examples of how donations to parties may result in undue influence or provide unbalanced access to decision makers.
2 Explain two potential problems with state funding of political parties.

Answers online

Left wing and right wing

Table 2.2 shows the main distinctions between left-wing and right-wing political ideas and ideals.

> **Left wing** Ideologies, ideas and policies that are associated with socialism, including redistribution of income, regulation of the excesses of capitalism, protection for workers' rights, a stress on state welfare and state control of some major industries.
>
> **Right wing** Ideologies, ideas and policies that promote free market capitalism and acceptance of social and economic inequality, and that advocate a limited role for the state, including low taxation and welfare levels, the promotion of free markets and a hard line on crime and, in relation to security and preventing terrorism, a preference for the collective rights of the community over individual human rights.

Table 2.2 Left- and right-wing political ideas

Left-wing ideas	Right-wing ideas
Redistributing income from rich to poor through taxation and welfare as well as a generous minimum wage.	Low levels of personal and corporate taxation to encourage private enterprise and to create incentives to work.
Strong support for the welfare state and opposition to private-sector involvement in the provision of such services.	Keeping welfare benefits relatively low as an incentive for people to find work and not become too dependent on the state. Extreme right-wing views include the replacement of the welfare state with private insurance.
Support for workers' rights and trade union power, and the protection of workers' rights in such areas as job security, fair contracts and good working conditions.	The state should not interfere with the working of the economy save for exceptional circumstances.
The state should run industries which are vital to society and the economy, typically energy, rail and the mail system.	Private enterprise would run key industries more efficiently than the state. Support for free markets in goods, finance and labour, including reducing trade union power.
Support for measures designed to create equality of opportunity, largely education, which is mainly funded by general taxation.	Promote a free market approach to education with an acceptance of private schooling.
A focus on equal rights for all groups in society, especially women and minorities.	A strong emphasis on law and order.
Support for aid to poorer countries.	A focus on national unity and patriotism.

Now test yourself

TESTED

3 Look at the policies described in the left-hand column of the table below. In each case state whether you think they are left wing, right wing or neither (i.e. centrist).

Policy	Left wing, right wing or centrist?
Nationalisation of the railways	
Raising the minimum wage well above the rate of inflation or the increase in earnings	
Reducing the rate of corporation tax levied on businesses	
Extending the rights of workers against unfair employment practices	
Extending the construction of nuclear power stations	
Increasing the level at which people start paying inheritance tax to £1 million	
Transferring local authority services into the private sector	

4 Outline two other policies not mentioned above which could be described as right wing and two which could be described as left wing.

Answers online

My Revision Notes: Pearson Edexcel A-Level Politics: UK politics second edition

The Conservative Party

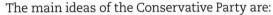

Main ideas

The main ideas of the Conservative Party are:
+ a stress on order and harmony in society
+ opposition to strongly held ideology or political principles
+ a preference for gentle reform over radical ideas
+ a belief in individualism and a limited state when it comes to economic matters
+ patriotism and support for traditional institutions and values
+ a pragmatic approach to political decision making
+ low taxation, financial responsibility and support for capitalism
+ a stress on the importance of private property ownership
+ a preference for community rights over individual rights when it comes to fighting terrorism
+ a stress on law, order and national security

However, the Conservative Party is not completely unified. The two main party factions are described below.

> **Party faction** A group within a political party, either formal or informal, which promotes ideas that are significantly different from the mainstream ideas of the party.

One Nation Conservatives

The One Nation faction tends to:
+ believe in *noblesse oblige*
+ accept the need for the welfare state
+ believe in the organic society — this involves support for local institutions (the Church etc.) that One Nation Conservatives see as the key to binding society together
+ be pro-EU
+ encourage private enterprise although accepts the 'mixed economy'

> **One Nation** A faction within the Conservative Party that is concerned with social cohesion. As a result, it is supportive of the welfare state and advocates a mixed economy rather than one that solely promotes privatisation.
>
> **Noblesse oblige** A French expression that essentially means that the rich have responsibility to the poor.

New Right Conservatives

The New Right faction tends to:
+ believe that individual wealth should not be taxed
+ believe that the welfare state leads to a dependency on the state
+ have a respect for order — a strong police force is required
+ be wary of immigration, be anti-EU and pro-America
+ have a strong belief in a limited state — in favour of privatisation

It should be noted that the New Right is itself divided into two sub-factions, neo-conservatism and neo-liberalism.

> **New Right** A faction within the Conservative Party that combines neo-conservative beliefs (traditional values and an emphasis on law and order) with neo-liberal beliefs (limited state intervention in the economy and low taxation).

> **Neo-conservativism** emphasises a belief in order and traditional values, and a wariness of immigration. Neo-conservatives primarily focus on the structure of society and the political system. They believe that society is naturally hierarchical.
>
> **Neo-liberalism** places greater emphasis on limited government intervention in the economy. Free markets and privatisation are promoted while welfare is opposed due to the fear that it leads to dependency.

Now test yourself

5 Decide whether the policies listed below would be supported by One Nation Conservatives or New Right Conservatives.

2019 Conservative manifesto promises	New Right or One Nation?
Promise not to raise income tax, VAT or national insurance	
Australian-style points system to control immigration	
20,000 more police and tougher sentences for criminals	
50,000 more nurses and 50 million more GP surgery appointments a year	

Answers online

Is the Conservative Party a One Nation or a New Right party?

REVISED ◯

Table 2.3 outlines the evidence as to whether the Conservative Party currently supports One Nation or New Right policies and ideas.

Table 2.3 Does the Conservative Party support One Nation or New Right policies and ideas?

Policy area	New Right evidence	One Nation evidence
Economy	The 2019 manifesto promised not to raise national insurance contributions, VAT and income tax. *These policies fit in with the belief that people should keep their wealth.*	Chancellor Rishi Sunak announced a £170 billion investment programme in the 2020 budget, which included a number of infrastructure projects, in a bid to boost economic growth. *This policy fits with the One Nation belief in a mixed economy with some state intervention.*
Welfare	Since 2010 the party has supported welfare reform, which has led to a reduction of benefits through benefit caps, the 'bedroom tax' and the introduction of universal credit. *These policies support the view that welfare leads to dependency, and that market-based solutions to service provision are preferable.*	The 2019 manifesto spoke of 'levelling up' funding for schools and hospitals, with Boris Johnson promising 20,000 more police officers and 50,000 more nurses. *These policies support the One Nation view of noblesse oblige — that the rich have responsibility for the poor.*
Law and order	In 2020, the home secretary, Priti Patel, proposed a points-based immigration system to reduce unskilled migration. Boris Johnson promised to end the early release of those found guilty of terror-related offences after the London Bridge and Streatham attacks. *These policies fit with the New Right belief in a strong police force and in respect for order and people knowing their place in the hierarchy.*	David Cameron favoured rehabilitation instead of punishment for drug addicts. Furthermore, Theresa May warned the police about the overuse of stop and search against people from minority ethnic groups. *Both of these policies fit with the One Nation belief in compassionate conservatism.*
Foreign affairs	Boris Johnson promised to 'get Brexit done' in the 2019 general election. The Tories supported the US-led wars in Afghanistan and Iraq, and believe that terrorism is a clear and present threat to the nation. *These positions fit in with the New Right dislike of the EU and support for the US–UK special relationship.*	Most Conservative MPs at the time voted and campaigned to remain in the EU. *This position fits in with the pro-EU stance of One Nation Conservatives.*

The Labour Party

Main ideas

The main ideas and aims of the Labour Party are:
+ to reduce inequality in society
+ a progressive tax system to redistribute real income
+ relatively high direct taxes to fund public services
+ support for an extensive, well-funded welfare state, including a free healthcare system and comprehensive education
+ measures to reduce poverty, especially child poverty
+ to regulate capitalism
+ a belief in the power of the state to promote social and economic reform
+ to balance the interests of workers against those of employers
+ to promote equal opportunities and reduce unjustified privilege
+ the promotion of equal rights

However, the Labour Party is not completely unified. The two main party factions are described below.

Left-wing 'Old Labour' (or social democracy)

The Old Labour faction believes in the following:
+ greater social equality through redistribution
+ that the rich should be taxed more than the poor
+ an active role for the state, where key industries should be controlled by the government and the workers should benefit from the money these industries make
+ a focus upon rehabilitation when it comes to criminal justice and crime
+ favouring of diplomacy and resolving disputes through peaceful means

> **Old Labour** The faction of the Labour Party that supports traditional socialist principles. These include greater social equality, an active role for the state in the economy and generous welfare provision.

Centrist 'New Labour' (or Third Way)

The New Labour faction believes in the following:
+ Redistribution from the rich to the poor is not a priority, so long as there is equality of opportunity.
+ There should be a mixed economy, whereby the government controls some public services while most of industry is controlled by private investors.
+ Where possible, there should be public–private partnerships when it comes to providing services such as health and education.
+ Diplomacy does not always work — sometimes military intervention on humanitarian grounds is necessary.
+ While it is important to consider the causes of crime, it is also necessary to have a strong criminal justice system with tough sentencing.

> **New Labour** The centrist faction in the Labour Party that promotes equality of opportunity rather than absolute equality and that advocates a mixed economy. It is comfortable with private involvement in welfare provision.

Now test yourself

6 Decide whether the policies listed below would be supported by 'Old Labour' or 'New Labour'.

2019 Labour Party manifesto	'Old' or 'New' Labour?
Immediately suspend the sale of arms to Saudi Arabia for use in Yemen	
Increase income tax for those earning over £80,000 per year	
Bring water and energy companies into public ownership	

Answers online

Is the Labour Party still a socialist party?

Table 2.4 looks at whether the current Labour Party retains the socialist, left-wing 'Old Labour' beliefs or has adopted more moderate 'New Labour' ideas.

Table 2.4 The Labour Party: 'Old Labour' beliefs or 'New Labour' ideas?

Area of discussion	Evidence of centrism (New Labour)	Evidence of socialism (Old Labour)
Equality	The gap between the richest and poorest grew under the last Labour government, even though it introduced the minimum wage. *This evidence fits with the New Labour belief that redistribution of income is not a priority, so long as there is equality of opportunity.*	The 2019 Labour Party manifesto pledged to raise the minimum wage from £8.21 to £10 per hour while also raising taxes on high earners. *This policy fits with the socialist belief in equality and that the rich should be taxed the most, the poor the least.*
Economy	Labour did not reverse Thatcher's privatisation of public utilities when in government. *This policy fits with the New Labour idea of a mixed economy.*	The Brown government nationalised (took over) failing banks including Northern Rock and part of the Royal Bank of Scotland. Corbyn pledged to create a national investment bank with over £350 billion coming from the public purse to support the rebuilding of regional industries. *Labour's recent policies support an active role for the state, with key industries controlled by the government.*
Welfare	Cleaning services in the NHS were 'contracted out' to private companies under the last Labour government. The party also supported encouraging businesses to sponsor underperforming schools. *This policy fits with the New Labour preference for public–private partnerships when it comes to running the welfare state.*	Under Corbyn, Labour promised to take hospital cleaning back into public hands. Furthermore, the party's 2019 manifesto promised to bring the delivery of education back into local authority control, away from academy chains. *This policy reversal fits with the Old Labour scepticism of private involvement in the running of the welfare state.*
Law and order	The 2019 manifesto promised to restore prison officer numbers to 2010 levels and recruit more frontline police officers to prevent crime. *This policy fits with the New Labour focus on being 'tough on crime, tough on the causes of crime'.*	The 2019 manifesto proposed 'a presumption against prison sentences' for non-violent and non-sexual offences. *This policy fits with the Old Labour belief that prison isn't the only way to ensure that an offender can be rehabilitated.*
Foreign affairs	Former Labour leader Ed Miliband supported tough action against ISIS. Hilary Benn, Labour's former shadow foreign secretary, voted in favour of action in Syria in 2015, demonstrating that a large part of the Parliamentary Labour Party remains some distance away from 'Old Labour'. *These examples show that, regardless of who is leader, the New Labour view that 'humanitarian intervention' is sometimes necessary, with or without international support, remains an influential one. Many Labour MPs accept that diplomacy does not always work.*	Miliband urged his party to vote against military action in Syria in 2013 and called for greater UN engagement. Corbyn similarly voted against action in Syria. *These stances fit with the socialist ideas of internationalism and making greater use of diplomacy before military action is considered.*

Remember

While many of Labour's 2019 manifesto commitments reflected 'Old Labour' ideas, there remained a degree of centrist influence. The Parliamentary Labour Party resisted many of Jeremy Corbyn's ideas and openly challenged his leadership. It is important to note that the left-wing Corbyn was replaced by the far more centrist Keir Starmer as leader.

Now test yourself   TESTED

7   Here are three arguments. Develop each of them with an example from this chapter.

Argument	Example to develop this argument
'The Labour Party under Jeremy Corbyn moved sharply to the left.'	
'Many of Labour's 2019 manifesto commitments reflected socialist principles.'	
'From 2020 "Old Labour" appears to be in retreat.'	

Answers online

The Liberal Democratic Party

Main ideas   REVISED

The main ideas of the Liberal Democratic Party are:
+ a strong belief in individual liberty
+ a stress on equal rights and the rule of law
+ state welfare to provide equal opportunities and greater freedom of choice, with a well-supported education system
+ checks and balances in the political system to prevent abuse of power
+ constitutional reform to make the UK more democratic and to decentralise power
+ greater protection for the environment and natural resources
+ support for private property ownership
+ the abolition of inherited privilege
+ an ease with people leading diverse lifestyles and with multiculturalism
+ a close relationship with the EU

However, the Liberal Democratic Party is not completely unified. The two main party factions are described below.

Classical ('Orange Book') liberals   REVISED

Classical liberals believe in:
+ maximisation of personal freedom, extended to freedom for individuals to keep their own wealth and property
+ free markets and free trade
+ a smaller state with curbs on government spending

Classical liberals Liberals following a form of liberalism harking back to the nineteenth century which proposed the maximisation of personal freedom and the minimal state.

34

Modern liberals

Modern liberals believe in:
- freedom being achieved by a strong welfare state that helps to provide equality of opportunity
- an 'enabling' state
- a graduated tax system whereby lower-income groups do not pay as much as higher-income groups

> **Modern liberals** Liberals who emerged after classical liberalism in the late nineteenth century. While still insisting on maximum freedom, they also accept that the state should intervene to create greater equality of opportunity, welfare and social justice. Modern liberals also support social diversity.

Table 2.5 examines whether the Liberal Democrats are a unified party.

Table 2.5 Are the Liberal Democrats a unified party?

2019 manifesto promise	Do classical liberals support the policy?	Do modern liberals support the policy?
Promise to tackle the climate emergency by insulating all low-income homes by 2025	Yes. This policy does not interfere with property rights and would therefore be supported.	Yes. Reducing energy bills means the low-paid will be more 'free' to save or to spend their wages on what they need.
Stop Brexit	Yes. Desire for free markets and free movement of capital leads classical liberals to support this policy.	Yes. Modern liberals believe that Britain's diverse, multicultural society will come under threat from Brexit.
Increase corporation tax to 20% from the current 17%	No. Higher taxes on businesses could harm growth.	Yes. It is important to raise taxes in order to fund the welfare state.
Reverse cuts to school funding and allow schools to employ 20,000 more teachers	No. Classical liberals supported the austerity agenda of the coalition government of 2010–15.	Yes. Education funding is key to ensuring equality of opportunity.

> **Remember**
>
> The 'Orange Book' faction was particularly influential when the party entered into a coalition with the Conservative Party between 2010 and 2015. Its leader at the time, Nick Clegg, said that the party needed to be 'savage' when it came to public-sector cuts. However, since 2015 the party has moved back towards supporting modern liberal policies, as Table 2.5 demonstrates.

> **Now test yourself** TESTED
>
> 8 Give two examples of modern liberal policies.
> 9 Give two examples of classical liberal policies.
>
> **Answers online**

The ideas, policies and impact of other parties

You should know the main political stance and impact of these other parties:
+ United Kingdom Independence Party (UKIP)
+ Brexit Party
+ Scottish National Party (SNP)
+ Plaid Cymru (Welsh Nationalists)
+ Green Party
+ Democratic Unionist Party (DUP) (Northern Ireland conservatives)
+ Sinn Fein (Northern Ireland Irish nationalists)

Table 2.6 shows the ideas and policies and the political stance of the other political parties in the UK.

> **Green New Deal** A set of proposals to create a more environmentally sustainable economy that also addresses structural inequality and poverty. Policies include measures to insulate homes and creating jobs in green industries such as wind turbine production.

Table 2.6 The policies and political stance of the other political parties in the UK

Party	Policies	Political stance
Scottish National Party	+ A second Scottish independence referendum + In the absence of independence, as much devolved power as possible, including on matters such as employment law + Close ties to the EU + End austerity by lifting benefit caps and halting universal credit + Strong support for public-sector health and education + Investment in renewable energy and support for a Green New Deal + Cancellation of the Trident nuclear missile programme	Left
Brexit Party	+ A 'clean break' Brexit + Abolish the House of Lords and reform the voting system + Oppose privatisation of the NHS + End the BBC licence fee + Caps on immigration	Right
UKIP	+ Complete withdrawal from the European Union + End the BBC licence fee + Caps on immigration + Increase in police numbers	Right
Green Party	+ Environmental protection with support for a Green New Deal + Support for a universal basic income + Close ties to the EU + Political reform, including changing the electoral system and lowering the voting age	Left
Plaid Cymru	+ Similar nationalist policies to the SNP but acceptance that Welsh independence is unlikely for many years + Similar economic and social policies to the SNP	Left
Democratic Unionist Party	+ Close ties between Northern Ireland and the rest of the UK + Keeping an open border with the Republic of Ireland after Brexit + Resistance to liberal social policies such as same-sex marriage + Opposition to integration of religious schools	Right
Sinn Fein	+ Reunification of Ireland + Raising the living wage + Northern Ireland to automatically re-enter the EU in the event of Irish reunification	Left

---

Now test yourself   TESTED ◯

10 Identify similarities between the smaller parties and the three main parties by completing the table below.

Party	One policy the party supports	Also supported by...
SNP		
Brexit Party		
Green Party	Electoral reform	Liberal Democrats

Answers online

The importance of other parties

Small and emerging parties in the UK can impact the outcome of elections and the policies of the three main parties, as shown in Table 2.7.

Table 2.7 How important are smaller parties in the UK?

Importance of smaller parties	Limits to importance
They may divert votes away from the main parties. Examples: the SNP has decimated Labour support in Scotland; UKIP took votes away from both the Conservatives and Labour in 2015.	Their support base might be limited to a specific region (e.g. the SNP in Scotland) and their electoral impact might be limited to one election (e.g. UKIP's vote collapsed in the 2017 general election).
When a constituency is marginal between large parties, small parties may split the vote one way or the other. Example: the Brexit Party did not campaign in marginal, Conservative-held seats in the 2019 election, allowing leave supporters to vote for the Conservative Party.	The first-past-the-post electoral system is not kind to parties whose vote is wide but shallow, rather than concentrated. Example: UKIP won nearly 13% of the vote in the 2015 general election but won only a single seat.
Small parties may affect the policies of large parties if they present an electoral threat. Example: UKIP's success at the 2014 European Parliamentary elections lead to a Conservative manifesto promise of an in–out referendum on EU membership. The Brexit Party's popularity at the 2019 European elections had a similar effect, encouraging the Conservatives to adopt a 'hard' Brexit stance.	The policies of the smaller parties are often subsumed by the larger parties, leaving them with limited appeal. Example: the Labour Party supported bringing forward the date for net-zero carbon emissions in its 2019 manifesto, dampening support for the Green Party.

Remember

The importance of small parties is not confined to how many seats they may win in representative assemblies. Small parties may threaten to win some of the votes normally cast for a large party. The policies of the larger parties might then be changed to head off this challenge.

Now test yourself

TESTED

11 Complete the table below by considering the limits of each specific party's influence.

Party	Why this party has been influential	Limits to influence
SNP	Its success in Scottish Parliamentary elections resulted in the Scottish independence referendum in 2014.	
Brexit Party	Its electoral threat led to the Conservative Party pushing for a harder Brexit in 2019.	
Green Party	It has kept the issue of climate change on the agenda, pushing larger parties to move faster towards net-zero emissions.	

Answers online

The UK party system

There are a number of ways of describing the UK party system. Several factors need to be considered, such as how many parties have a realistic chance of forming a government, how many have representation in a parliament or assembly, and how many have a significant impact on policy. Table 2.8 summarises a number of party system theories.

> **Party system** A reference to how many parties achieve representation and have an influence on the politics of a country.

Table 2.8 Theories of party systems

Type of system	Description
Dominant party	One party dominates the number of seats in the legislative body and is the only party in government.
Two-party	Only two parties have significant representation.
Three-party	Three parties have significant representation.
Multi-party	Four or more parties have a significant number of representatives elected and smaller parties have a significant impact on policy.

Evidence of a dominant party system

REVISED ●

+ The dominant party theory takes into account that usually only one party forms the government in the UK.
+ From 1979 to 2010 Britain had only one party in government (18 years of Conservative rule followed by 13 years of Labour rule).
+ The coalition that followed was a temporary phenomenon and since the 2015 election it has been business as usual.
+ One party (the Conservatives) is in government; since the 2019 general election the Tories have had 56% of the seats in the House of Commons.
+ Even a minority government is able to control the agenda of Parliament; Theresa May was able to delay votes on Brexit to the time of her choosing.
+ A weak government can therefore still dominate Parliament — the Conservatives were able to survive a no-confidence vote in January 2019.

Counter-arguments

+ The Conservative government in Westminster between 2017 and 2019 relied on the DUP for key votes in order to pass legislation.

Evidence of a two-party system

REVISED ●

+ First-past-the-post (FPTP) ensures that only two parties, Labour and Conservative, have a realistic chance of winning the general election.
+ FPTP ensures the two-party system is maintained in terms of how votes are converted into seats.
+ In 2017, the Labour and Conservative parties won 580 of the 650 seats (89%).
+ In 2019, they won 568 of the 650 seats (87%).

Counter-arguments

While it is easier to make the case for a two-party system in Westminster, especially in terms of votes and seats, the picture elsewhere is far more complex:
+ The SNP controls the Scottish government.
+ Labour formed a coalition with the Liberal Democrats in Wales after the 2016 Welsh Assembly elections.
+ Northern Ireland has its own parties that make up the Northern Irish Assembly, including Sinn Fein and the DUP.

These examples can be explained by the different electoral systems used in regional and sub-national elections that benefit smaller parties.

Evidence of a three-party or multi-party system

REVISED ●

+ In 2019 some 82 MPs were elected from outside the two main parties and now enjoy representation in Parliament, compared to an average of 9 between 1950 and 1970.
+ The Green Party has its first MP — Caroline Lucas represents Brighton Pavilion and she has increased her majority in the last three general elections.
+ In the 2019 general election, the SNP won 48 seats in the House of Commons, making it comfortably the third largest party in terms of seats.

Counter-arguments

+ The FPTP electoral system doesn't allow for a permanent multi-party system and more often than not benefits the two larger parties.
+ The 2017 general election saw the highest vote share for the two major parties since 1970, at 82.3%. In 2019 this vote share only fell back to 75.8%.
+ The Lib Dem revival in 2019 was muted.

Table 2.9 shows the percentage of votes won by the main parties from 1979 to 2019.

Table 2.9 A decline in two-party dominance?

General election year	% of votes won by the two main parties
1979	80.8
1983	70.0
1987	73.0
1992	76.3
1997	73.9
2001	72.4
2005	67.6
2010	65.1
2015	67.2
2017	82.3
2019	75.8

Exam tip

Think about party representation across the country and in the various regional parliaments and assemblies. Don't just focus on Westminster.

Now test yourself   TESTED ⬤

12 Give three arguments in favour of there being a two-party system.

13 Give three arguments against the view that there is a two-party system.

Answers online

Factors affecting party success

Much of the material relating to the success or otherwise of parties is contained in Chapter 4 on voting behaviour, along with information about the role of the media. The following are key elements in parties' fortunes:

+ **Quality of leadership:** this includes the following qualities which are known to attract support:
  + experience
  + decisiveness
  + ability to lead
  + media image
  + intelligence
  + apparent honesty
+ **Valence:** this refers to how people generally view the party's image. It includes such issues as:
  + how competent they were when they were last in office
  + how economically responsible they appear to be
  + whether they are trustworthy
  + how unified they are — parties that are disunited tend to fare badly at elections; conversely, united parties are usually successful
+ **The influence of the press:** the broadcast media have a legal requirement to be neutral. Media influence therefore centres on the press. The main aspects of press influence on the fortunes of parties are as follows:
  + The press presents significant images of party leaders as being weak or strong, decisive or indecisive, charismatic or unpopular.
  + By publishing opinion poll data, they may influence voting behaviour.
  + Newspapers have preferences for particular parties and may present the policies of their favoured parties in a more positive light.
  + At election time most newspapers recommend that their readers vote for a particular party.

Making links

When looking at the success and failure of parties, you should also revise material in Chapter 4 on voting behaviour. You will need to expand your answers on media influence to include the recent impact of social media (also covered in Chapter 4).

Table 2.10 provides examples of how different factors can affect the success of political parties.

Table 2.10 How different factors can affect the success of political parties

Factor	Positive effects upon party success	Negative effects upon party success
Quality/perceptions of leadership	In 1997, Tony Blair's high approval rating helped his party to a landslide victory.	In 2019, a poll conducted by Opinium found that 43% of respondents who did not vote Labour chose not to do so because of their negative perceptions of Jeremy Corbyn, the Labour Party leader.
Valence/party image	In 1983 and 1987, a divided Labour Party was heavily defeated by a united Conservative Party under Margaret Thatcher.	In 1997, the Conservatives were divided over Europe and lost heavily to Labour, which was united around Tony Blair's New Labour agenda.
Influence of the press	In 1997, the *Sun* shifted its allegiance, pronouncing that 'The Sun backs Blair'. Subsequently, the party enjoyed positive headlines in the run-up to the general election, helping it to win.	In 1992, the *Sun* ran with the headline that if Labour leader Neil Kinnock won the election, 'will the last person to leave Britain please turn out the lights'. After the election result, which returned a majority Conservative government, the tabloid claimed that 'It's The Sun wot won it'.

Now test yourself

TESTED ⬤

14 Give an example for each factor below that affects the fortunes of political parties.

Factor	Example
Quality of leadership	
Valence	
The press	

Answers online

Exam practice

1 Evaluate the view that small parties have an enormous impact on UK politics today. [30]
2 Evaluate the view that the funding of parties should be controlled and reformed. [30]
3 Using the source, evaluate the view that the Conservative Party has abandoned New Right policies and ideas. [30]

While the Conservative Party has indeed been consumed by Brexit since the 2016 referendum, there have been indications of a shift away from New Right policies. Theresa May appeared to distance herself from Margaret Thatcher and from the aggressive individualism that characterised the 1980s. Economically, May pledged to end austerity and focus on the issues of the 'just about managing' and to end the 'burning injustices' that exist, particularly among minority groups. The 2019 Conservative Party leadership race was notable for the spending commitments that several candidates made on education and in other areas of the public sector. It appeared that at long last the Conservative Party had found that 'magic money tree' whose existence they had denied for so long. The 2019 election manifesto contained pledges to 'level up' the country and increase spending on the NHS.

➔

Answers and quick quizzes at **www.hoddereducation.co.uk/myrevisionnotesdownloads**

However, it would be wrong to say that the Conservative Party has turned its back on the New Right, especially with its continued preference for low taxes. It is still wary of the welfare state, as its 2017 manifesto showed, with a promise to means-test winter fuel allowances and to take into account people's assets (notably houses) when determining the costs they would need to pay for elderly care. Labour and the media soon labelled this a 'dementia tax', and the prime minister announced a seeming U-turn within 24 hours, stating that the total

amount would be capped. Furthermore, the manifesto pledged to remove the triple-lock on pensions, which further raised the concerns of elderly voters. The shadow of Brexit continues to loom large, as does the party's panicked response to the anti-immigrant sentiment of the Brexit Party and UKIP. These 'little Englander' views find a good degree of sympathy among Tory Party activists.

Source: original material

In your response you must:
+ compare the different opinions in the source
+ consider this view and the alternative to this view in a balanced way
+ use knowledge and understanding to help you analyse and evaluate

Answers and quick quiz 2 online

Exam skills

For the source question, it is important to first decide whether you agree or disagree with the statement in the question. Then you should use two different-coloured highlighter pens to identify arguments in the source that you agree with and arguments that you disagree with. You should then plan your essay by creating a quick table like the one shown below, which includes three source

arguments from each side of the debate. Even though you will choose a side that you support, you should still aim to provide examples for both sides of the argument.

The table shows a sample plan for the source-based question above, where the student has decided to argue against the view that the Conservative Party has abandoned New Right ideas and policies.

Source argument I disagree with	Evidence that is used to justify this argument	Source argument I agree with	Evidence and examples from my own knowledge to support this argument
'The 2019 election manifesto contained pledges to "level up" the country and increase spending on the NHS.'	Promise of 50,000 extra nurses	'It is still wary of the welfare state'	Caps on housing benefit
There has been a move away from 'aggressive individualism'	Party introduced the furlough scheme to help workers during the Covid-19 pandemic	'Continued preference for low taxes'	Reduced income tax rates for high earners
Pledge to help the 'just about managing'	Minimum wage has been increased	Party's 'panicked response to the anti-immigrant sentiment'	Pledges to reduce immigration to the tens of thousands

Summary

You should now have an understanding of:
+ both the functions and features of political parties in the UK
+ the issues surrounding the funding of political parties
+ the ideas and policies of the three main UK parties
+ the factions within the main parties
+ the ideas and policies of small and emerging parties
+ the party system
+ the factors that determine the success or failure of parties

41

My Revision Notes: Pearson Edexcel A-Level Politics: UK politics second edition

3 Electoral systems

First-past-the-post (plurality system)

The main features of first-past-the-post (FPTP) are as follows:

+ The country is divided into constituencies.
+ Each constituency elects one Member of Parliament (MP).
+ Each party can nominate only one candidate to stand for election in each constituency.
+ Voters have only one vote each and they choose their candidate by marking an X next to their favoured candidate's name.
+ The winner of the election is the candidate who wins more votes than any other candidate. This is known as a plurality.
+ The winner does not require an absolute majority (50%+) of the votes cast.
+ This system is used for elections to the Westminster Parliament.

> **First-past-the-post (FPTP)** The electoral system used in UK general elections; the candidate with the most votes in a constituency wins a seat in the House of Commons.

> **Plurality** A term used to describe 'the most votes'. If a candidate receives a plurality then they have won more votes than any other candidate. That does not mean that they have received an 'absolute majority', which is what happens when a candidate wins 50%+ of the vote. Under FPTP, a winning candidate only requires a plurality of the vote, not an absolute majority.

The outcomes of first-past-the-post include the following:

+ Many seats are safe seats, which means that the same party wins the seat at every election and there is no realistic possibility that any other party could win the seat.
+ Only a minority of seats are marginal seats, which are seats where more than one party has a chance of winning.
+ The winning party often wins enough seats to govern on its own with a clear mandate; it tends to produce 'strong government'. However, the 2010 and 2017 general elections did not produce this sort of result.
+ It discriminates in favour of parties whose vote is highly concentrated in one area (if a party's vote is 'efficient'). This phenomenon allows the winning party to enjoy a winner's bonus.
+ It discriminates against parties whose vote is thinly spread throughout the country (those who secure only a few votes in each constituency).
+ Voters are more likely to engage in tactical voting.
+ FPTP is therefore associated with a two-party system.

> **Safe seat** A constituency where one party is so dominant that it is almost unthinkable that it will not win the seat at every election.
>
> **Marginal seat** A constituency where more than one party has a realistic chance of winning the seat at an election and the outcome of the election is likely to be close.
>
> **Winner's bonus** First-past-the-post tends to reward those parties whose votes are highly concentrated and 'efficient', winning just enough votes in each constituency to win multiple seats. This phenomenon leads to the largest party having a disproportionate seat share compared to their national share of the vote.
>
> **Tactical voting** When voters choose a candidate who might not have been their preferred choice in order to keep the candidate they least like from winning.

Table 3.1 provides an assessment of FPTP.

Table 3.1 An assessment of first-past-the-post

Advantages	Disadvantages
FPTP usually produces a single clear winner that can form a **majority government**, with a clear mandate to govern. Example: the Conservative Party won a commanding majority at the 2019 general election, winning a mandate to 'get Brexit done'.	FPTP does not always guarantee a clear winner and by extension a clear mandate. Example: in 2010 and 2017 FPTP failed to give an absolute majority to any party but delivered a **hung parliament** instead. The Conservative Party had to form a **coalition** with the Liberal Democrats between 2010 and 2015 and govern as a **minority government** between 2017 and 2019.
It produces one single representative for each constituency and so creates a close constituency–MP bond, with MPs gaining a reputation for standing up for constituents. Example: in 2019, Jess Phillips MP stood outside a school in her Birmingham Yardley constituency to defend teachers who taught primary school children about LGBTQ+ relationships.	The overall outcome is not proportional or fair. Some parties win more seats than their overall support warrants while others win fewer than they deserve. Example: the Liberal Democrats won almost 12% of the vote in the 2019 general election but just under 2% of the seats.
Accountability of the individual MP is clear to the electors. Example: several MPs who represented constituencies that voted to leave the EU lost their seats at the 2019 general election after the MPs campaigned for a second referendum.	It means that many votes are effectively wasted because they can have no impact on the outcome in safe seats. Many seats become part of party 'heartlands' where there is no possibility of a realistic challenge from other parties. It also produces 'electoral deserts' where there is effectively no party competition.
It helps to prevent 'extremist' parties from breaking into the system. Example: the British National Party received over half a million votes in the 2010 general election but failed to win a seat.	It prevents new parties breaking into the system and so produces political 'inertia'. Example: UKIP won broad support across the country in the 2015 general election with almost 4 million votes, yet it only secured one seat.
The system helps to reflect regional differences in voter preferences. Example: the SNP is strong in Scotland, the Labour Party is strong in inner cities and the Conservative Party's popularity is reflected by how many rural seats the party wins.	Votes are of unequal value in that votes in safe seats are less valuable than votes in marginal seats. Example: the Electoral Reform Society estimated that almost three-quarters of votes in the 2015 election either went to losing candidates or were surplus to what the winning candidate needed to gain a plurality.
Voters are faced with a simple choice — they simply place a cross next to their preferred candidate.	It encourages tactical voting among some voters and so they abandon the party they really want to support. Example: the Electoral Reform Society estimated that some 6.5 million voters engaged in tactical voting in the 2017 election.

Majority government One party is in power and enjoys a majority of seats in the House of Commons.

Hung parliament Occurs when no party has a majority of seats; either a minority government or a coalition government is formed.

Coalition government Where two or more parties are in power. While no party enjoys a majority of seats on their own, combining the seats of the parties in power gives them a majority of seats overall.

Minority government One party makes up the government, but it does not have a majority of seats. It often governs by making deals with other parties to support it on key votes, which is what the Conservatives did with the DUP between 2017 and 2019. Such deals are called 'confidence and supply' arrangements.

Figure 3.1 provides a summary of FPTP.

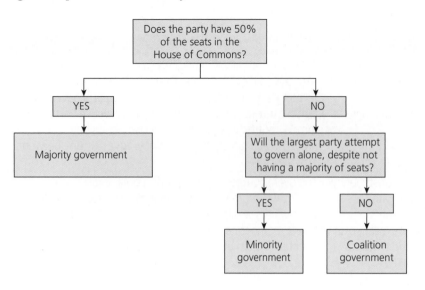

Figure 3.1 Summary of first-past-the-post

Now test yourself   TESTED ⬤

1 Describe three advantages of first-past-the-post.

2 Describe three disadvantages of first-past-the-post.

Answers online

The supplementary vote (majority system)

The main features of the supplementary vote (SV) system are as follows:

+ Each voter gets two votes — a first and second preference.
+ There are two rounds of counting.
+ In the first round, the first-preference votes are counted. If no candidate gets 50% of the first-preference votes, then a second round of counting begins.
+ In this second round, all candidates apart from the leading two are eliminated. The second-preference votes for the eliminated candidates are then transferred to the candidates still left in.

This system is used to elect a number of city and regional mayors, including the London mayor (Table 3.2).

Supplementary vote (SV)
An electoral system used to elect the London mayor and one that attempts to ensure that the winning candidate receives as close to 50% of the vote as possible. Voters have two votes — a first and second preference.

Table 3.2 The 2021 London mayoral election (candidates receiving 1% of the vote and above)

Candidate	% vote after the first round of counting	% vote after the second round of counting
Sadiq Khan (Labour)	40	55.2
Shaun Bailey (Conservative)	35.3	44.8
Siân Berry (Green Party)	7.8	Eliminated
Luisa Porritt (Liberal Democrat)	4.4	Eliminated
Niko Omilana (Independent)	2.0	Eliminated
Lawrence Fox (The Reclaim Party)	1.9	Eliminated
Brian Rose (London Real Party)	1.2	Eliminated
Richard Hewison (Rejoin EU)	1.1	Eliminated
Count Binface (Count Binface Party)	1.0	Eliminated

The outcomes of the supplementary vote (SV) system include the following:

+ Fewer votes are wasted than under FPTP. For example, Green Party voters knew that their second-preference vote might count even if their first one didn't.
+ The system promotes a two-horse race. In the 2021 mayoral election, the Green Party candidate, Siân Berry, was eliminated because she received only 7.8% of the vote.
+ Alliances with other parties are critical. Sadiq Khan won many second-preference votes from Green votes after promising to adopt environmentally friendly policies.
+ The British National Party (BNP) won just over 13,000 votes in the 2016 mayoral election but non-moderate parties have little chance of winning under SV.
+ By having a second preference, voters are able to choose a candidate they 'don't mind'. This is why the BNP could never win, because very few people would say they 'don't mind' the BNP.
+ In this respect, SV ensures that the 'least hated' candidate wins.

Table 3.3 gives an assessment of the SV system.

Table 3.3 An assessment of the supplementary vote system

Advantages	Drawbacks
The winning candidate can usually claim to have an overall majority of support.	SV still promotes a two-party system, as smaller parties have little chance of winning.
It is relatively simple for voters to understand.	The winning candidate may win on second choices despite being behind on the number of first preferences they received.
Voters' first and second choices are relevant.	It can still result in wasted votes if a voter does not choose either of the candidates who make it to the second round of counting.

> **Remember**
>
> The supplementary vote is, broadly speaking, a majoritarian rather than a proportional system. In a proportional system, an attempt is made to ensure that the percentage of votes a party receives is reflected in the percentage of seats they are awarded. In a majoritarian system, attempts are made to ensure that the winning candidate receives as close to an absolute majority as possible, usually by having a second round of voting (as in the French presidential elections) or a second round of counting (as with the supplementary vote).

The additional member system (hybrid system)

The additional member system (AMS) operates in elections to the Scottish and Welsh Parliaments and the Greater London Assembly. It is a hybrid between first-past-the-post and proportional representation (PR).

AMS works like this:

+ Each voter has two votes — one for a candidate and one for a party (see Figure 3.2).
+ Each constituency elects one candidate (using FPTP), whereby voters choose their preferred candidate. Two-thirds of the seats are allocated in this way.
+ The other third of the seats are elected on the basis of closed regional list voting, whereby voters have an additional vote to select their preferred political party.
+ This is where the country is divided into regions and each party offers a list of candidates for each region.
+ Seats awarded from the party list system are adjusted to give a more proportional result (using a complicated formula called the D'Hondt method).
+ Simply put, parties that do less well in the constituencies have their proportion of list votes adjusted upwards.
+ Those that do proportionally well under first-past-the-post have their list votes adjusted downwards.
+ The overall effect is to make the total result close to proportional of the total votes cast.

> **Additional member system (AMS)** An electoral system used for a number of elections in the UK, including the Scottish and Welsh Parliamentary elections. AMS maintains elements of FPTP, specifically the use of constituencies.
>
> **Proportional representation (PR)** A description of any electoral system that awards seats broadly in proportion to the votes cast for each party.

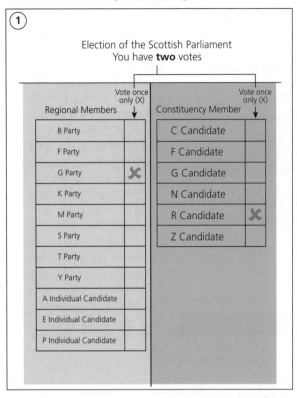

(a) Scottish Parliamentary elections using AMS

① Election of the Scottish Parliament
You have **two** votes

(b) Scottish local elections using STV

② Election of Council A, Z Ward
Instead of using a cross, number the candidates in the order of your choice.

Put the number 1 next to the name of the candidate who is your first choice, 2 next to your second choice, 3 next to your third choice, 4 next to your fourth choice and so on.

You can mark as many or as few choices as you like.

Party C	Candidate A	4
Party D	Candidate D	
Independent	Candidate H	1
Party A	Candidate J	2
Party F	Candidate Q	
Party E	Candidate S	
Party B	Candidate W	3
Party A	Candidate Z	

Figure 3.2 Examples of voting in AMS and STV systems

The outcomes of the additional member system include the following:
+ The overall outcome tends to be approximately proportional to the votes cast.
+ AMS usually denies parties a large majority of seats. This is why the SNP has had to run minority governments in Scotland and why Labour has frequently entered into coalitions in Wales.
+ Small parties can win seats even though they do not have a chance of winning any constituencies. UKIP won its first seats in the Welsh Assembly in 2016.
+ There are two types of representative — a constituency representative and a party list representative.
+ The party list representatives have taken on leadership roles more easily because they have fewer distractions (like constituents) to contend with.
+ Coalitions have been relatively stable.
+ A minority of voters 'split their ticket' by voting for one party in the constituency vote but a different party in the list part of the system.

Table 3.4 provides an assessment of AMS.

Remember

Many students think that proportional representation is an electoral system. It is not. Proportional representation is a description applied to a number of systems which have proportional outcomes, such as the single transferable vote (STV) system, which will be explained later in this chapter.

Table 3.4 An assessment of the additional member system

Advantages	Drawbacks
It produces a broadly proportional outcome and so is fair to all parties.	It produces two classes of representative — those with a constituency and those elected through the lists. The latter tend to be senior.
It gives voters two votes and so more choice.	It is more complex than first-past-the-post. Having two votes can confuse some voters.
It combines preserving constituency representation with a proportional outcome.	It can result in the election of extremist candidates.
	It is more likely to result in minority or coalition government.

Now test yourself

TESTED ⬤

3   Detail the impact or outcome of AMS in three bullet points.

4   Describe the way in which AMS compensates parties that fare badly in
    constituency elections.

Answers online

The single transferable vote (proportional system)

The single transferable vote (STV) system is used in Northern Ireland and
in Scottish local government elections. It operates in this way (see also
Figure 3.3):

+ There are six seats available in each constituency.
+ Each party is permitted to put up as many candidates as there are seats in
  a constituency (i.e. up to six).
+ Voters put the candidates in their order of preference by placing a number
  (1, 2, 3 etc.) beside their names.
+ Voters can choose candidates from different parties if they wish.
+ Winning candidates are elected by reaching a quota that is calculated by
  using this formula: VOTES ÷ SEATS + 1.
+ So, if 100 votes were cast and five seats are available, the quota is 100 ÷ 5 + 1.
  This works out as 21.
+ Successful candidates must equal or surpass this number of votes.
+ At first all the first preferences are counted for each candidate. Any
  candidates who achieve the quota are elected automatically.
+ If no one reaches the quota then the candidate with the least first
  preferences is eliminated and the second and subsequent choices of the
  voters who chose that candidate are transferred.
+ If a candidate does reach the quota, the second and subsequent
  preferences from the ballot papers of the elected candidates are added to
  the other candidates. If this results in another individual achieving the
  quota, they are elected.
+ This process continues until six candidates have achieved the quota and
  are elected.

> **Single transferable
> vote (STV)** A proportional
> electoral system that is
> used for Northern Irish
> Assembly elections and
> Scottish local elections.
> Constituencies are of a
> larger size than under
> FPTP and elect several
> representatives rather
> than just one. Voters rank
> candidates in order of
> preference. To get elected,
> a candidate must receive a
> set number of votes, known
> as a quota.

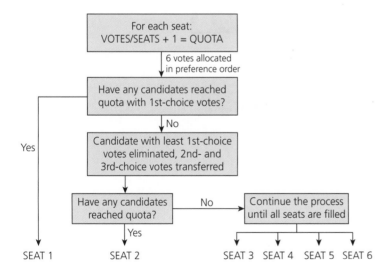

Figure 3.3 The STV system

The outcomes of the single transferable vote system include the following:

+ The overall outcome is largely proportional to the first-preference votes cast for each party.
+ It results in a multi-party system.
+ STV encourages power sharing so coalitions are the norm. In Northern Ireland this is between divided communities.
+ STV — and the coalitions it promotes — can result in gridlock. For instance, Sinn Fein and the DUP were unable to come to a compromise and form a coalition between 2017 and 2020.
+ STV has broken the link between a single representative and their constituents.
+ The complex nature of STV has confused voters, as happened with Scottish voters in 2007, when they voted using STV for local elections but also voted using AMS for Scottish Parliamentary elections.

Table 3.5 provides an assessment of STV.

Table 3.5 An assessment of the single transferable vote system

Advantages	Drawbacks
Voters have a simple choice — it's 'as easy as 1, 2, 3'.	Calculating the result is very complex and takes a long time.
It produces a broadly proportional outcome.	It is more likely to result in minority or coalition government that could be unstable.
It gives voters a wide choice of candidates. Their second and subsequent choices are taken into consideration in the counting.	It can help candidates with extremist views to be elected.
As there are six representatives per constituency, each voter has a choice of those to represent them and usually they find themselves represented by someone from the party they supported.	With six representatives per constituency, the lines of accountability are not clear.

Exam tip

While it is really useful to understand how different electoral systems work, you are not expected to give lengthy descriptions of how AMS, STV and SV operate. Instead, you should focus more on their impact and the strengths and weaknesses that have been outlined in the tables in this chapter.

Now test yourself TESTED

5 Give three reasons why STV may seem too complex.
6 Which electoral systems are being described in the table below?

Description	Electoral system
An electoral system that regularly, although not always, produces a government with a working majority in the UK Parliament	
An electoral system that allows voters to discriminate between candidates of the same party	
An electoral system which tries to ensure that the winner is supported by an absolute majority of voters	
An electoral system that gives voters two votes	
An electoral system that features both constituencies and proportional representation	

Answers online

Impact of electoral systems on voter choice

Table 3.6 summarises how each electoral system used in the UK affects voter choice.

Table 3.6 Electoral systems and voter choice

Electoral system	Effect on voter choice	Where it is used
First-past-the-post	Voters choose one candidate only.	UK general elections
Supplementary vote	Voters have a first and second preference.	London mayoral election
Single transferable vote	Voters rank candidates in order of preference (1, 2, 3 etc.).	Northern Ireland Assembly and Scottish local elections
Additional member system	Voters have two votes, one for a candidate to represent their constituency and one for a political party.	Scottish and Welsh Parliamentary and Greater London Authority elections

Electoral systems, types of government and party systems

Various electoral systems tend to produce different forms of government and promote specific party systems, as shown in Table 3.7. (For more details of party systems, see Chapter 2.)

Table 3.7 Electoral systems, the forms of government they produce and party systems they promote

Electoral system	Type of government typically formed	Party system typically promoted
First-past-the-post	Single-party majority government (with the 2010–15 Parliament a notable exception)	Dominant party if the winning party enjoys a substantial winners' bonus or two-party if the majority is much smaller
Supplementary vote	Single candidate becomes mayor	Two-party (because only two candidates can make it through to the second round of counting)
Additional member system	Two-party coalition government or one-party minority government (with the 2012–16 majority Scottish government a notable exception)	Dominant party (the SNP has dominated Scottish Parliamentary elections) or three-party (smaller parties have participated in government, including the Liberal Democrats in Wales)
Single transferable vote	Power sharing among several parties	Multi-party

> **Now test yourself**   TESTED
>
> 7 Describe two effects of AMS upon the party system and the type of government that it tends to produce.
> 8 Describe two effects of STV upon the party system and the type of government that it tends to produce.
>
> **Answers online**

First-past-the-post compared with other systems

Table 3.8 shows first-past-the-post compared with alternative systems on the basis of various objectives.

Table 3.8 First-past-the-post compared with alternative systems

Objective	Most appropriate system
Strong, stable government	First-past-the-post
Maximum voter choice	Single transferable vote
A multi-party system	Single transferable vote
Strong constituency representation	First-past-the-post
A proportional outcome	Additional member system
An absolute majority for the winner	Supplementary vote
Votes are of equal value	Single transferable vote

Electoral reform

Table 3.9 presents the arguments for and against changing the electoral system for general elections in the UK, by comparing FPTP with the other systems mentioned in this chapter.

Table 3.9 Arguments for and against electoral reform

Arguments in favour of retaining FPTP	Arguments in favour of electoral reform
FPTP tends to produce decisive results and strong and stable government. It also maintains a strong constituency link between MPs and voters. + While the 2010 and 2017 general elections did not provide a decisive victory for one party, such results are rare. + The 2019 general election delivered an 80-seat majority for the Conservative Party, ending the uncertainty around Brexit. + The constituency system ensures clear representation for citizens.	Electoral reform is necessary because FPTP delivers disproportional results. + In 2015, roughly 5 million Green and UKIP voters were effectively disenfranchised, with their parties winning only one MP each. + FPTP discriminates against parties whose vote is thinly spread throughout the country but rewards those parties whose vote is concentrated in enough places to win several seats. + Voters are therefore forced to vote tactically. + Many votes are wasted, particularly in 'safe seats'. + UK general elections produce governments that do not enjoy the support of a majority of the electorate. In 2005, 2010 and 2015, the winning party failed to achieve 40% of the popular vote.
SV does not solve all of the problems of FPTP. + Minor parties still have little chance of winning. + With one exception (Ken Livingstone in 2000), only Labour and Conservative candidates have ever gone through to the second round of counting in London mayoral elections. + Tactical voting is still an issue, just as under FPTP.	SV wastes fewer votes. + Many Green Party voters chose Labour candidate Sadiq Khan as their second preference in the 2016 London mayoral election. This support proved decisive in Khan's eventual victory after the second round of counting. Green Party voters knew that their second preference vote might count even if their first one didn't. + SV tends to ensure that the 'least hated' candidate wins because it seeks to propel the winning candidate as close to 50% of the vote as possible.

Answers and quick quizzes at **www.hoddereducation.co.uk/myrevisionnotesdownloads**

Arguments in favour of retaining FPTP	Arguments in favour of electoral reform
AMS often fails to give one party a decisive majority, unlike FPTP. ✦ The SNP is now running the government in Scotland, as a minority government — this means the party does not have a majority of seats. ✦ Labour is running a minority government in Wales — this means that it is the largest party but it still does not have over 50% of the seats so needs to get support from other parties to get measures through the Parliament.	AMS allows smaller parties a chance to influence decision making. ✦ The Liberal Democrats have frequently participated in government in both Scotland and Wales. ✦ Coalitions have been relatively stable — all have thus far lasted the full term. ✦ AMS retains the constituency link, since two-thirds of seats are allocated using FPTP.
STV can lead to confusion and gridlock. ✦ Between 2017 and 2020 in Northern Ireland, neither Sinn Fein nor the DUP was able to form a coalition or work together. The UK government therefore had to impose a budget on the province. ✦ STV has broken the link between a single representative and their constituents, as STV involves creating large constituencies that have several representatives.	STV requires the sharing of power between different parties, therefore resulting in 'grown-up' politics. ✦ It is perhaps the model for a country that is divided over Brexit and where there are a number of nations and regions attempting to retain their identity. ✦ Having large constituencies with a number of representatives means that the whole community is better served. A Labour MP, for example, might take up different issues in the constituency from a Conservative. ✦ Voters have a wide choice of candidates to choose from.

Exam tip

Make sure you can quote plenty of statistics from recent elections, both general and devolved, in order to illustrate the effects of various electoral systems and to be able to compare them.

Now test yourself

TESTED ◯

9   Look again at the arguments for and against retaining FPTP and complete the sentences in the right-hand column on alternatives to FPTP.

Argument for retaining FPTP	Argument for replacing FPTP
STV can lead to gridlock, so FPTP should be kept.	STV is better because…
AMS is not better than FPTP because it often fails to give the winning party a majority of seats.	AMS is better because…
In FPTP the winning candidate only requires a plurality of votes, making it a much simpler system than SV.	SV is better because…

Answers online

How referendums have been used in the UK

You should know the details of several referendums to illustrate your answers. Table 3.10 outlines some of the key UK referendums.

Table 3.10 Important referendums in the UK since 1997

Year	Issue	Level	Why held	Yes (%)	No (%)	Turnout (%)
1997	Should additional powers be devolved to Scotland and a Scottish Parliament be established?	Scotland	A fundamental change in the system of government needed popular consent.	74.3	25.7	60.4
1997	Should additional powers be devolved to Wales and a Welsh Assembly be established?	Wales	A fundamental change in the system of government needed popular consent.	50.3	49.7	50.1
1998	Should the Belfast Agreement be implemented?	Northern Ireland	This agreement required support across the whole divided community.	71.7	28.9	81.0
2004	Should additional powers be devolved to northeast England and a regional assembly established?	Northeast England	To test support for devolution in England.	22.1	77.9	47.7
2011	Should the UK adopt the alternative vote system for general elections?	National	A referendum on this issue was contained in the coalition agreement at the insistence of the Liberal Democrats.	32.1	67.9	42.2
2014	Should Scotland become a completely independent country?	Scotland	A fundamental question about who governs Scotland, which gained traction after the SNP became the majority party in the Scottish Parliament.	44.7	55.3	84.6
2016	Should the UK remain a member of the EU?	National	The governing Conservative Party was split on the issue and sought to meet the electoral challenge of UKIP.	48.1	51.9	72.2

> **Remember**
>
> To make best use of Table 3.10, it is important to examine the turnout in these referendums. The vote on changing the electoral system in 2011 received only a 42% turnout. You can use this example to show that referendums do not always increase participation.

The reasons why referendums have been held in the UK include:
+ An issue might be divisive within government and/or within the nation, so a referendum can settle the issue and unite the population. Example: the referendum on the Belfast Agreement in Northern Ireland in 1998.
+ An issue may be of huge constitutional significance and so require the direct consent of the people. Example: the 2014 referendum on Scottish independence.
+ It helps to entrench and safeguard constitutional changes. This may be necessary when the community requires reassurance that the change is permanent. Example: the 1997 referendum on creating a Scottish Parliament.
+ To judge public opinion on an issue, especially where a change in taxation may be involved. Example: the referendum on whether to establish a North East Assembly in 2004.

The impact of referendums in the UK

It can be argued that some referendums have a huge impact on politics and wider society, while others have only minor consequences. Some examples are shown below.

Answers and quick quizzes at **www.hoddereducation.co.uk/myrevisionnotesdownloads**

Referendums that had a significant impact:

+ The 2014 referendum on Scottish independence appeared at first to have settled the issue. There was a high turnout and a decisive result. However, the continued dominance of the SNP in Scottish politics means that a future referendum on Scottish independence could still be held.
+ The 2016 EU referendum shocked the political world. It has resulted in the biggest diplomatic upheaval since the Second World War and revealed that the country was deeply divided on its future direction. These divisions in turn affected general election results.

Referendums that had only a minimal impact:

+ Voters rejected the establishment of a North East Assembly in 2004. While this result slowed the pace of devolution, it has arguably not prevented other areas from creating new political institutions, most notably the Greater Manchester Combined Authority.
+ The 2011 referendum on electoral reform produced a decisive result though on a low turnout. The issue of electoral reform is still not seen as particularly important by most voters.

> **Exam tip**
>
> When discussing and analysing the use of referendums, avoid giving examples only from one referendum, such as the referendum on EU membership. Giving a variety of examples will improve the quality of your answer.

The case for and against referendums

The case for and against the continued use of referendums is a balanced one. The main issues include those shown in Table 3.11.

Table 3.11 An assessment of the use of referendums

Arguments for	Arguments against
Referendums are the purest form of democracy, uncorrupted by the filter of representative democracy. They demonstrate the pure will of the people, as shown in the EU vote. They are a direct expression of popular consent.	The issue may be too complex for people to comprehend. The electoral system, which was the subject of the 2011 referendum, was difficult for voters to understand.
Referendums can help to unite a divided society, as occurred with the decisive result of the 1998 vote on the Belfast Agreement.	Referendums are designed to heal divisions but can sometimes cause them. The EU referendum exposed deepened divides between nations (Scotland voted to remain while England voted to leave) and between age groups (only 27% of 18–24-year-olds voted to leave the EU compared to 60% of people aged 65+). There was also an increase in racial tension, with police forces reporting rises in race-related hate crimes following the referendum.
Referendums can solve conflicts within the government and the rest of the political system. This was especially the case with the EU referendums in both 1975 and 2016.	Excessive use of referendums may undermine the authority of representative democracy, which has been a particular danger in some states in the USA. In California, a number of referendums have prevented lawmakers from raising taxes which has resulted in frequent budget crises. If similar referendums were held in the UK, they would likely have the same effect.
Referendums are particularly useful when the expressed (as opposed to implied) consent of the people is important, so that the decision will be respected. This was very true of the votes on devolution in 1997.	A referendum can represent the 'tyranny of the majority'. This means that the majority that wins the vote can use their victory to force the minority to accept a change that is against their interests. The Scots, Northern Irish and Londoners, who voted strongly to stay in the EU in 2016, claimed they were being tyrannised by the English majority.
People have access to many sources of information and can use this to make more informed decisions than they could in the past.	Voters may be swayed by emotional rather than rational appeals. They may also be influenced by false information. In the EU referendum in 2016, the Leave campaign claimed that withdrawing from the EU would result in a saving of £350 million per week which could be spent on the NHS.
	Some questions should not be reduced to a simple Yes/No answer; they are more complicated.

10 Provide counter-arguments to the arguments made in the table below.

Referendums are beneficial because they...	Counter-arguments
educate the public	
solve conflicts within the government	
help unite a divided society	

Answers online

Revision activity

1 List three referendums that in your view had an immense political impact. Remember to give reasons why.

2 Give three arguments for and three arguments against the wider use of referendums, giving examples to develop your points.

3 Describe the impact, both negative and positive, of the 2016 EU referendum.

Exam practice

1 Evaluate the view that referendums undermine representative democracy in the UK. [30]

2 Evaluate the view that electoral systems used in the UK promote multi-party politics. [30]

3 Using the source, evaluate the view that the Westminster electoral system (first-past-the-post) should be retained. [30]

The continued use of the first-past-the-post (FPTP) electoral system for Westminster elections has aroused controversy for decades. More than half of MPs typically do not command majority support within their constituency. At the national level, FPTP regularly produces governments elected on a minority of the popular vote. This feature means that significant numbers of voters feel that the system lacks legitimacy. FPTP does not translate the number of votes into seats for each party with any real accuracy. The system favours parties whose vote is concentrated, rather than those whose support is spread across a large geographical area. FPTP produces another kind of distortion known as 'electoral deserts': areas of the country where one party cannot win seats. FPTP limits the choice for voters in several ways. The overall impact of FPTP is the depression of voter turnout and the increased likelihood of tactical voting.

However, the ease and familiarity of FPTP help to explain continuing public support for its retention. The relatively small size of most FPTP constituencies, and the fact that a single MP is responsible for representing those who live within the constituency, are often seen as strengths. At general elections it usually gives a clear majority of seats to one party, which then has a mandate to carry out its programme. Supporters of FPTP also point to the problems with the alternatives: proportional systems boost the significance of smaller, perhaps extremist parties, allowing them to hold the balance of power. Furthermore, proportional representation is far more likely than FPTP to produce unstable coalition governments.

Source: original material

In your response you must:
+ compare and contrast the different opinions in the source
+ examine and debate these views in a balanced way
+ analyse and evaluate only the information presented in the source

Answers and quick quiz 3 online

When approaching an essay, make sure that you focus on the question and what you are being asked. It is worth considering the points outlined below. Consider the following question:

Evaluate the view that referendums undermine representative democracy in the UK.

What you need to do is not as simple as stating all the arguments for and against referendums. The arguments that you use must be relevant to representative democracy. Therefore, it is best to detail the features of representative democracy and then to examine how referendums might affect them. Below is an essay plan that could help you.

Introduction

✦ Define key word: 'undermine'. For example:
In the context of referendums, representative democracy might be 'undermined' if accountability is affected, if the rights of minority groups are threatened, and if elected politicians no longer have the flexibility to take tough decisions.

Main body

✦ Three paragraphs that contain arguments and counter-arguments. Themes: accountability, safeguarding rights of minority groups, election of representatives.
✦ Start each paragraph with the side that you least agree with (e.g. do not undermine) and end the paragraph with the side of the argument that you most agree with (e.g. do undermine).
✦ The table below gives an outline of the possible content you could use for each paragraph.

Paragraph theme/features of representative democracy to be discussed	How referendums do not undermine representative democracy	How referendums undermine representative democracy
Accountability	They can act as a form of protest.	It is difficult to reverse the result of a referendum or to hold a great mass of people responsible for the decisions they themselves have made.
Safeguarding rights of minority groups, providing social representation	They provide a voice to specific regions on specific issues.	They can result in the tyranny of the majority, discounting the views of the minority.
People elect representatives to take decisions on their behalf.	Referendums give clear instructions to decision makers on what people want them to do.	They undermine the room for manoeuvre for politicians to take decisions in the national interest.

Conclusion

✦ Remind the examiner of the direction you took at the start. For example:
While there are legitimate arguments to show they are beneficial, referendums ultimately undermine representative democracy more than they help it.
✦ Repeat the judgements made throughout. For example:
It is clear that referendums weaken or blur the lines of accountability. They can negatively affect the rights of minority groups and they limit the room for manoeuvre that politicians have to take decisions in the national interest.

You should now have an understanding of:
✦ the workings of first-past-the-post
✦ the workings of the supplementary vote system
✦ the workings of the additional member system
✦ the workings of the single transferable vote system
✦ the impact of all the electoral systems described above, and the specific advantages and disadvantages of each

✦ how the formation of governments and the party system are affected by different electoral systems
✦ the arguments for and against the introduction of proportional representation for general elections
✦ several recent referendums used in the UK, including the reasons for them being held
✦ the arguments for and against referendum use

Questions on voting behaviour typically focus on the factors that affect the way people vote. It is important to be able to analyse the significance of the following:

+ social and demographic factors (class, age, region etc.)
+ valence (image) issues and economic voting
+ party leaders
+ the idea that voters make a rational choice when casting their ballot
+ the campaign and party manifestos
+ tactical voting
+ turnout
+ the role of opinion polls
+ the media

In your answers you should include examples from a range of general elections, specifically: (a) the 1997 election, (b) one election from the period 1945–92 and (c) one election after 1997. Case studies of three elections have been provided at the end of this chapter to help you.

Social and demographic factors affecting voter behaviour

When we examine social or demographic factors, we consider whether a person's social class, age, ethnicity and gender affect their voting, and whether there are any regional influences upon voting decisions.

Social class

Social class is one of the factors to be considered in relation to voting behaviour. Table 4.1 shows a system often used in the UK to divide people into social classes.

> **Social class** The classification of people based on their occupations and, to some extent, their income. Social class is often expressed using social grades AB, C1, C2 and DE, which divide the population up into different professions.

Table 4.1 How people are grouped into social classes in the UK

Classification	Description	Typical occupations
AB	Higher and intermediate managerial, administrative and professional occupations	+ Banker + Doctor + Company director + Senior executive
C1	Supervisory, clerical and junior managerial, administrative and professional occupations	+ Teacher + Office manager + IT manager + Social worker
C2	Skilled manual occupations	+ Plumber + Hairdresser + Mechanic + Train driver
DE	Semi-skilled and unskilled occupations, unemployed and lowest-grade occupations	+ Labourer + Bar staff + Call centre staff + Unemployed

Source: 2011 census

How important is social class in determining the way people vote?

+ Peter Pulzer once wrote that 'Class is the basis of party politics, all else is embellishment and detail.'
+ Traditionally, the AB groups described in Table 4.1 would largely vote Conservative, while the DE groups would largely vote Labour. They would do so based on perceptions that those parties would best represent their interests.
+ In the 1964 general election, Labour won 64% of DE voters while 78% of AB voters chose the Conservatives.
+ However, class dealignment has resulted in partisan dealignment, affecting the importance of social class in determining electoral outcomes. Table 4.2 demonstrates that the story of social class and voting is one of steady decline in its influence.

Class dealignment A trend whereby fewer people associate themselves with belonging to a particular social class, decreasing the impact of class on voting behaviour.

Partisan dealignment A trend whereby fewer voters are committed to, or loyal to, a specific party.

Table 4.2 Voting by social class

Election year	% class AB voting Conservative	% class DE voting Labour
1964	78	64
1997	41	59
2017	43	47
2019	45	39

Source: Ipsos MORI

Table 4.3 presents arguments regarding the importance of class-based voting.

Table 4.3 Importance of class in determining voting behaviour

Social class is important	Social class is not important
+ Class divides in voting might be expressed in other, more subtle ways, such as the probability that black and minority ethnic (BME) voters in low-paid jobs might vote Labour, or that DE voters in Kent might vote Conservative. + Education might be the new reflection of class, with 58% of those with GCSEs or below voting Conservative and 43% of those with a degree or higher voting Labour in the 2019 general election. + Equally, class plays a significant role in how political parties fight campaigns — the Tories targeted the 'left-behind towns' in 2017 and 2019.	+ In the 21st century, class-based voting has been undercut by class dealignment and issue-based voting (e.g. Brexit). + In the 2017 general election, the DE vote was split: 43% of this group voted Conservative and 47% Labour. + In 2019, the Conservatives won support from all social grades, including AB and DE. + Class is therefore no longer as important, as there is no clear divide between how different social grades vote.

The significance of class-based voting can be evaluated as follows:
+ Class is no longer as reliable a predictor as it once was of how a person might vote.
+ It is important to note, however, that class-based voting may manifest itself through other characteristics, such as levels of education, which means that the significance of class in how a person votes cannot be completely discounted.

Exam tip

When it comes to evaluating social factors, you must consider trends in voting patterns. There are three main ways you can do this:

1 Consider the significance of a social factor from one election to the next one.
2 Consider the significance of a social factor across a number of elections (at least three).
3 Consider the significance of a social factor when compared to another — for example, comparing the importance of class with that of age.

You should aim to use all three measures.

1 Complete the table below, using data from three different general elections that have been mentioned so far to demonstrate the declining influence of class upon voting behaviour.

General election year	Data
1964	
2017	
2019	

Answers online

Age

REVISED ◯

While it is becoming more difficult to see class differences in how people vote, the age of a voter appears to be highly significant, particularly when considering the 2017 and 2019 general elections. Table 4.4 illustrates the effect of age upon voting behaviour.

Table 4.4 Effect of age upon voting behaviour

Age	2017 general election		2019 general election	
	% Con	% Lab	% Con	% Lab
18–24	27	62	21	56
70+	69	19	67	14

Source: YouGov, Ipsos MORI

The significance of age-based voting can be evaluated as follows:
+ Age has not always been as significant as it is today.
+ In 1983, 42% of 18–24-year-olds voted Conservative and 33% voted Labour. This age demographic was split in how it voted.
+ Yet by 2017, Labour enjoyed a majority of support from all age groups between 18 and 39.
+ According to YouGov, for every 10 years older a person was in 2019, the likelihood that they would vote Labour decreased by 8 points.
+ Meanwhile, the Conservatives enjoy substantial support among the over-60s, with 61% of the 65+ age group voting Tory in 2019.
+ The gap between how young people vote and how older people vote is therefore far greater than the gap between how AB and DE voters cast their ballot. Age has therefore replaced class as the most significant indicator of voting behaviour.
+ However, it must be noted that age has only appeared to be the most significant social factor for the past two elections — the next election will likely determine whether this trend continues.

Exam tip

To attain AO2 marks, you need to explain not only how people vote but why they vote the way they do. For example, when discussing why young people are more likely to vote for the Labour Party, you could consider the party's stance on tuition fees and its opposition to cuts in public services.

Region

REVISED ◯

Regional voting patterns appear to be significant. Table 4.5 shows the support for political parties and how this differs from region to region.

Table 4.5 Voting by region, 2019 general election

Region	% Con	% Lab	% Lib Dem	% SNP
Northeast	38.3	42.6	6.8	n/a
London	32.0	48.1	14.9	n/a
East Midlands	54.8	31.7	7.8	n/a
Southeast	54.0	22.1	18.2	n/a
Wales	36.1	40.9	6.0	n/a
Scotland	25.1	18.6	9.5	45.0

Source: House of Commons Library

In summary:

+ The Labour Party has strong support in London and a plurality of support in Wales and in the north of England.
+ The Conservative Party is strongly supported in the southeast of England. It also fares well in the east of England.
+ The SNP appears to dominate in Scotland.

Regional voting patterns and Brexit

Table 4.6 shows a strong correlation between how specific constituencies voted over Brexit and how voters in those constituencies cast their ballot in the 2019 general election, which demonstrates how specific issues might affect how different regions vote in general elections.

Table 4.6 Vote share change between the 2017 and 2019 general elections in constituencies where 60% or more voted to Leave or Remain in the 2016 EU referendum

Party	Strong Leave constituencies (% change from 2017 GE)	Strong Remain constituencies (% change from 2017 GE)
Conservatives	+6.1	−2.9
Labour	−10.4	−6.4
Liberal Democrats	+2.6	+4.7

Source: BBC

Table 4.6 clearly shows the following:

+ The pro-Brexit Conservative Party performed better in Leave areas than in Remain areas.
+ Labour, while performing poorly overall in 2019, did far worse in Leave-voting constituencies.
+ The Liberal Democrats, who campaigned to 'Stop Brexit', did better in Remain constituencies than in Leave constituencies.

Now test yourself TESTED

2 Give three statistics to show that where a person lives can affect how they vote.
3 Give three statistics to show that age plays an important role in determining how someone votes.

Answers online

Remember

Region plays an important part in the way people vote, but perhaps it is too closely linked to economic conditions and to class to be considered the sole determinant of voting behaviour. Now that the UK has left the EU, it is difficult to determine how important the issue of Brexit will be in perpetuating regional voting patterns.

Gender REVISED

+ Gender appears to have little or no impact on voting intentions.
+ In 2019, 46% of men and 44% of women voted Conservative while 31% of men and 35% of women voted Labour. These statistics show that there is not a gaping gender divide in how people vote, as roughly similar proportions of men and women voted Conservative, and the same was the case for Labour.
+ A clear gender divide appears to exist only among 18–24-year-olds, where 65% of women voted Labour compared to 46% of men.
+ Yet both men and women in this age group still voted more heavily for Labour than Conservative in 2019 and so it is difficult to untangle the significance of age from that of gender.

Ethnicity REVISED

Ethnicity is a major predictor of how a person will vote. Table 4.7 shows that black and minority ethnic (BME) voters are far more likely to vote for Labour than for other parties. Meanwhile, recent elections have also shown that white voters are more likely to vote for the Conservative Party.

4 Voting behaviour and the media

My Revision Notes: Pearson Edexcel A-Level Politics: UK politics second edition

Table 4.7 Ethnicity and voting: patterns for BME voters

Election	% BME voting Conservative	% BME voting Labour	% BME voting Liberal Democrat
2010	16	60	20
2015	23	65	4
2017	19	73	6
2019	20	64	12

Source: Ipsos MORI

Table 4.8 analyses the influence of ethnicity upon voting patterns.

Table 4.8 Significance of ethnicity in voting patterns

Ethnicity is significant	Ethnicity is not significant

+ In 2015, the Conservatives enjoyed an 11-point lead over Labour among white voters and this increased in 2019 to 19 points.
+ Labour has maintained its support from BME voters over successive elections, receiving 64% of votes from BME voters in 2019 compared to only 20% for the Tories.
+ Minority ethnic voters tend to favour Labour, which stems from two historical reasons:
  + the anti-immigration sentiment of Conservative figures such as Enoch Powell and Norman Tebbit
  + the concentration of ethnic minority groups in urban industrial centres such as London, Birmingham and Manchester
	+ Research has showed that the BME community is complex in its voting patterns, and that religious factors may play a bigger role. Hindu and Sikh communities appear to vote in higher numbers for the Conservatives.
	+ The concentration of BME voters in lower-paid jobs might mean that support for Labour owes more to economic and class factors than to ethnicity.
	+ Likewise, the fact that many Asian Hindu voters have become wealthier over time might explain a bias towards the Tories.

Now test yourself

4 Give two reasons why voting behaviour could be better explained by other factors rather than ethnicity.

Answers online

TESTED ⬤

Exam tip

When considering the voting behaviour of specific social groups, it is important to use non-definitive language, such as 'usually', 'often' and 'tend to', since no group is completely homogeneous in its voting habits. BME voters tend to vote Labour. Equally, when explaining the reasons for social groups voting the way they do, use phrases like 'can be explained by' or 'might be…', as voting behaviour is not an exact science.

Non-social factors and voting behaviour

Valence

REVISED ⬤

Valence is one of the key factors that affects voting behaviour:
+ Valence concerns the general image of a party and its leader.
+ Valence is closely tied to the trust voters have in a governing party, or in an opposition party wishing to form the government. We sometimes refer to this as governing competency.
+ Valence can relate to trust on a specific issue or on a range of issues.

Governing competency A general feeling among voters that a party is either very competent in governing or much less competent. Competency refers largely to sound economic policies, sensible foreign policy and decisiveness in office.

Table 4.9 provides examples of how valence issues have affected general election campaigns.

Table 4.9 How valence issues have affected general election campaigns

Type of valence issue	Explanation	Examples
Governing competency	+ Does the government appear to be decisive? + Did the party govern well when it was last in power?	+ The Conservatives lost office in 1997 partly due to issues around competency, including the 'cash for questions' and 'mad cow disease' scandals.
Economic competence	+ How well did the party manage the economy last time it was in power?	+ The governing Conservative Party won the 1987 election, taking credit for the booming economy. + The Labour Party failed to convince voters in 2019 that it could pay for its spending plans.
Party unity	+ How united is the party? + Voters trust united parties but not disunited ones.	+ The Conservatives lost elections in 2001 and 2005 partly because they remained divided over the issue of Europe. + Division was also a serious problem for Labour in the 2017 general election, after Jeremy Corbyn faced a leadership election in 2016.
Image of leaders	+ Are the leaders admired and trusted?	+ The Liberal Democrats did well in 2010 because leader Nick Clegg was liked and respected. + Nevertheless, he lost respect after that and was heavily defeated in 2015.

Now test yourself TESTED ◯

5 Give examples of prominent valence issues affecting the outcomes of the general elections listed below.

Election	Valence issue
1987	
1997	
2019	

Answers online

Remember

Do not assume that the outcome of elections depends solely on the performance and image of the governing party. The image of the opposition is of almost equal importance.

Party leadership

REVISED ◯

Leaders who are unpopular tend to drag down a party's share of the vote, while popular leaders usually help their party's fortunes at the ballot box. But how important is party leadership in determining the outcome of general elections? Table 4.10 focuses on the debate around this issue.

Table 4.10 Party leadership and election outcomes

Leadership does affect the electoral outcome	Leadership does not affect the electoral outcome
Tony Blair: The Labour Party leader's high approval ratings propelled Labour to big election wins in 1997 and 2001, but Blair's waning popularity after the Iraq War correlates to Labour's reduced majority after the 2005 general election.	Clement Attlee: The Conservative Party leader and wartime prime minister, Winston Churchill, said of Attlee that he was 'a modest little man with much to be modest about'. Yet Labour under Attlee won a landslide victory in 1945.
Jeremy Corbyn: A 2019 survey of former Labour voters found that 43% of respondents cast their vote on the basis of 'leadership', perhaps highlighting how dislike of Corbyn helped shatter the so-called 'red wall', former Labour-held safe seats that were won by the Conservatives.	Margaret Thatcher: Labour's James Callaghan had higher net approval ratings than Margaret Thatcher in 1979, but her Conservative Party still won back power.

My Revision Notes: Pearson Edexcel A-Level Politics: UK politics second edition

Salience

REVISED

Salience concerns the identification of 'salient' or very important issues at stake in the election. Many voters are influenced by such salient issues, so parties often make them the main elements in their election campaigns. Below are some examples of salient issues that seem to have affected voting behaviour.

+ 2019: the issue of Brexit and whether voters preferred a second referendum or Boris Johnson's 'oven-ready' deal to 'get Brexit done'
+ 2010: the issue of the deficit and public finances, and whether there would be public-sector cuts or tax rises to address the problem
+ 1979: the issue of trade union power after a winter of industrial unrest

> **Remember**
>
> It is important to consider other explanations for electoral outcomes, even if an issue was particularly salient. In 2019, for example, while the issue of Brexit was important, so too were valence issues, specifically around Labour's manifesto commitments.

> **Now test yourself**   TESTED
>
> 6 Describe three salient issues that may have had an impact upon voting behaviour.
> 7 Look back at the sections on valence issues, leadership and salience. List three potential reasons why Labour lost the 2019 general election.
>
> **Answers online**

Party manifestos and election campaigns

The general election campaign refers to the period of time between the dissolution of Parliament (when the election is officially called) and the election day itself. Election campaigns typically last between 4 and 6 weeks. During this period, political parties each release a party manifesto. If elected, the winning party claims a mandate to introduce the policies that it contains.

It is the conventional wisdom that both the general election campaign and the release of a party manifesto rarely affect the outcome of the election, but as Table 4.11 illustrates, both the campaign and the manifesto can be significant in specific circumstances.

> **Manifesto** A set of commitments produced by each party at the start of an election campaign.
>
> **Mandate** The authority, granted by the people at elections, of the winning party at a general election. The newly elected government has the authority to carry out its election proposals contained in the party manifesto.

Table 4.11 Arguments concerning the significance of general election campaigns and party manifestos for electoral outcomes

Election year	The campaign and manifesto were important	The campaign and manifesto were less important than other, long-term factors
1979	Margaret Thatcher ran a disciplined campaign and utilised the clever slogan 'Labour isn't working' to depict rising unemployment.	Valence issues played a more prominent role. The Labour government was blamed for the 'winter of discontent'.
1997	Labour ran a cautious election campaign to maintain its poll lead. The party manifesto reflected Tony Blair's popularity by having his image on its front cover.	Tony Blair had positioned Labour to appeal more to middle-class voters, a process that took place long before the general election campaign.
2017	The Conservative Party was forced into a U-turn on its manifesto commitment to reform health and social care, after its policy was dubbed the 'dementia tax'. Opinion polls narrowed thereafter.	The salient issue of Brexit affected voting patterns far more than the 6-week election campaign or party manifesto launches.
2019	Labour's copious manifesto pledges led to questions of affordability.	The Conservative Party enjoyed a sizeable poll lead in the run-up to the campaign and questions of Corbyn's leadership had plagued the Labour Party for several years.

Tactical voting

When voters in UK general elections feel that their first-choice vote will be wasted because it is for a party that has no chance of winning, they may change their vote to their second choice. These voters go against their usual instincts and vote for a candidate from a party that has the best chance of beating the candidate they most dislike.

+ Typically, supporters of the Green Party may vote Labour to prevent a Conservative candidate from winning.
+ Meanwhile, a UKIP or Brexit Party voter may vote Conservative to keep Labour from winning.

The significance of tactical voting and its effect upon voting behaviour and electoral outcomes is considered in Table 4.12.

Table 4.12 Tactical voting and its significance

Tactical voting is important	Tactical voting is not important
+ The Electoral Reform Society estimates that 6.5 million voters 'held their noses' in the 2017 general election and voted tactically. + Websites such as SwapMyVote have allowed for more precise tactical voting. These sites allow two voters in different constituencies to make an informal agreement to cast a vote for one another's preferred party. + Election expert John Curtice estimates that tactical voting could have affected the outcome in 77 constituencies in the 2015 general election.	+ In 2019, Liberal Democrat voters appeared less willing to cast their vote for Labour candidates than in 2017, resulting in a loss of several marginal seats for Labour. + Attempts to persuade people to vote tactically often fail — the SNP won handsomely in Scotland in 2015 despite attempts by opposition parties to unite behind the same pro-union candidates. + Parties seldom issue formal advice to voters on voting tactically.

Turnout and electoral outcomes

The level of turnout can influence the outcome of an election because different demographic groups usually demonstrate different turnout levels. Younger people tend to demonstrate greater levels of disillusionment and apathy. The 2015 and 2017 elections show the importance of turnout in determining general election outcomes:

+ In 2017 the so-called 'youthquake', an increase in turnout among young voters who were energised by the leadership of Jeremy Corbyn, helped Labour reduce the gap between itself and the Conservative Party and may have denied Theresa May a parliamentary majority.
+ In 2015 higher turnout appeared to come from disillusioned Tories who 'came back home' after fears that Labour and the SNP would form a 'coalition of chaos'.

Turnout The percentage of the electorate that casts a vote.

Disillusion and apathy Traits that force down levels of turnout. They may be the result of low esteem for the political class or a general lack of interest in politics and a suspicion that politics cannot change things for many people.

Factors that affect turnout

REVISED

Table 4.13 considers the factors that may affect turnout in general elections.

Table 4.13 Factors affecting turnout

Factors that affect turnout	Example
Closeness of election	Many voters felt that the result of the 2001 general election was a foregone conclusion and Labour would win in another landslide. As a result, turnout fell to 59%. Yet in 1992, the closeness of the election saw a 78% turnout.
The choice between the two major parties	In 2017 the Labour Party offered a radically different manifesto from the Conservative Party, which may have encouraged young people to vote in greater numbers.
Salient issues	The issue of Brexit may have encouraged voters on both sides of the debate to vote for candidates and parties who supported their position, ensuring turnout in 2017 was the highest since 1997.

> **Remember**
>
> You need to be able to discuss the reasons why people do not vote and which people do not vote, almost as much as why people do vote. This issue is discussed more in Chapter 1.

> **Now test yourself**
>
> 9 Give two examples where higher turnout appears to have affected the outcome of an election.
>
> **Answers online**
>
> TESTED

Opinion polls

Opinion polls are carried out by research organisations using a sample of typical voters. They are mainly used to establish voting intention. They can also be used to assess leaders' popularity and the salience (importance) of specific issues. The main debates surrounding opinion polls centre upon the following:

+ whether their use during a general election campaign may affect how people eventually cast their ballot
+ whether the accuracy of opinion polls can be trusted
+ their role in affecting party policy

The influence of opinion polls in affecting party policy and voting behaviour is considered in Table 4.14.

Table 4.14 The influence of opinion polls upon voting behaviour and party policy

Opinion polls are influential	Limits of opinion poll influence
Their results may shape the way people cast their vote. + 1992: Most polls suggested that Labour would win the general election, which may have encouraged wavering, undecided voters to back the then Conservative government out of fear of a Labour administration led by Neil Kinnock. + 2015: The closeness of the polls led to Conservative efforts to warn about the possibility of a Labour–SNP coalition, which may have helped shift the election in favour of a small Tory majority. Opinion polls seem to influence party policy. + Polls showed that immigration became an important issue to voters after 2010, hence successive Conservative pledges to limit net migration to the 'tens of thousands'.	Opinion polls have proven to be inaccurate. + 2017: Most polls predicted a comfortable Conservative majority and didn't pick up the 'youthquake', an increase in younger voters who were prepared to turn up at voting booths and vote for Labour candidates. + 2016 EU referendum: The polls indicated that the Remain side would win and yet it didn't. Opinion polls may be affected by party policy rather than the other way around. + Arguably, Labour's manifesto in 2017 shifted and shaped opinion on public spending.

Answers and quick quizzes at **www.hoddereducation.co.uk/myrevisionnotesdownloads**

The debate over whether opinion polls should be banned in the lead-up to general elections has gathered traction. In France election polls are banned on polling day and the day before. Table 4.15 considers the debate as to whether the findings of opinion polls should be published before elections.

Table 4.15 Should the publication of opinion polls be banned in the run-up to elections?

For banning them	Against banning them
They may influence the way people vote. If the polls are showing a clear outcome one way or another, that might discourage people from voting at all.	It would infringe the principle of freedom of expression.
They have proved to be inaccurate, so they mislead the public. Some may have voted to leave the EU as a protest, as they expected the outcome would be 'Remain' and their vote would not matter.	If they are banned, they will still continue to be available privately for organisations that can afford to pay for them.
Arguably politicians should not be slaves to changing public opinion as expressed in the polls, which may in any case be inaccurate.	Polls give valuable information about people's attitudes, which can help politicians respond to their concerns.
Multiple countries ban the release of opinion polls, including countries such as Canada and France, which have similar political and democratic systems to the UK.	They would probably still be published abroad and people could access them through the internet.

Now test yourself   TESTED ◯

10 Give two arguments in favour of banning the publication of opinion polls in the run-up to general elections.

11 Give two examples, each for a different election, to show how opinion polls may have affected voting behaviour.

Answers online

The role and impact of the media in elections

When considering the role the media play in UK general elections, it is important to consider the following:
+ the role of media bias, specifically in the press
+ the role of television and specifically TV appearances by the leaders, including their participation in debates
+ the increased use of social media

The press
REVISED ◯

Most national newspapers in the UK support the Conservative Party, including those newspapers that have the highest circulation. The *Daily Mail*, the *Sun*, the *Daily Express*, the *Daily Telegraph* and *The Times* all have a Conservative Party bias, to a greater or lesser extent. The *Daily Mirror* and the *Guardian* generally support the Labour Party. The examples contained in Table 4.16 help us to analyse the influence of the press and whether newspapers persuade voters in such a way as to affect electoral outcomes.

> **Remember**
> Do not assume that opinion polls are always wrong. They build into their research a degree of tolerance, usually 3–4% either way, so if they are less than 4% out with their prediction they have been reasonably accurate.

Table 4.16 Press influence in three general elections

Election year	Press influence	Limits to press influence
1979	The *Sun* headline 'Crisis, what crisis?' at the height of the 'winter of discontent' suggested Labour leader James Callaghan was out of touch with ordinary voters and swung opinion against the formerly popular prime minister.	Perhaps the 1979 result is better explained by valence issues surrounding Labour's inability to handle industrial relations.
1997	The *Sun* switched support from the Conservatives to Labour. Tony Blair courted media mogul Rupert Murdoch, and subsequently much of the Murdoch-owned press switched allegiance.	The press was simply reacting to the prevailing mood of the time, reflected in the polls, which was clearly swinging towards Labour.
2017	According to YouGov, some 74% of *Daily Mail* readers voted Tory in 2017, demonstrating the influence of that paper's right-wing bias upon its readers.	The press barrage against Corbyn didn't work and failed to persuade enough voters to back the Tories. Despite the *Sun*'s 'Don't chuck Britain in the Cor-bin' headline and the *Daily Mail*'s 15-page anti-Labour spread the day before polling day, Labour saw its largest increase in vote share since 1945.

Press influence between elections

To assess the influence of the press, it is important to consider how media reporting may shape the policies of the major political parties. Below are some examples of how the press has influenced party policy:

+ In his first term in office, Blair sought to hold a referendum on joining the euro but abandoned this plan in the face of hostility from the Murdoch-owned press.
+ The *Daily Mail*'s campaign to seek justice for British-Jamaican teenager Stephen Lawrence in the early 1990s pushed the government into accepting an independent inquiry that found the Metropolitan Police to be institutionally racist.

However, press influence in between elections should not be overstated:

+ Leaders of political parties arguably have the most influence over their party's policies. Under Corbyn, the Labour Party appeared to have given up on trying to court the right-wing print media, adopting policies that were completely at odds with the Murdoch press, such as nationalising rail and the utility companies.
+ Political parties are complex organisations and formulate policies by taking on board the views of a range of different groups both inside and outside the party structures, including think tanks and pressure groups. For example, the Conservative Party's plans on universal credit were influenced heavily by the Centre for Social Justice, a think tank headed by former work and pensions secretary Iain Duncan Smith.

Remember

Do not assume that readers agree with the political stance of the newspaper they read. According to YouGov, 41% of voters who read the *Sun* did not vote Tory in 2017. Also, people may choose to read a paper that reinforces existing beliefs rather than read a paper that challenges their ideas.

Now test yourself TESTED ○

12 Complete the table below by considering the limits to press influence.

Election year	Limits to press influence
1979	
1997	
2017	

Answers online

Television and TV debates

The role that television plays in election campaigns usually relates to how a party leader comes across to viewers, in what is referred to as their televisual image. The examples in Table 4.17 help us to analyse just how important televisual image is in deciding electoral outcomes, especially in the era of TV debating.

> **Televisual image** How a leader comes across to voters on television, specifically how confident they appear in front of live television audiences and how well they perform in debates with other party leaders.

Table 4.17 Televisual image and electoral outcomes

A positive televisual image of the leader is important	A positive televisual image of the leader is not important
Neil Kinnock's triumphalist shrieking of 'We're all right' at the Sheffield Rally in 1992 may have put doubt in the minds of voters that he could be trusted to lead the country.	The Sheffield Rally happened only a week before the 1992 election and it is unlikely that this alone accounts for the different levels of support between the opinion polls and the election results.
The 2010 debate between the three main parties was credited with denying the Tories a parliamentary majority. Nick Clegg's strong showing and the resultant 'Cleggmania' raised his profile at the expense of David Cameron's, resulting in a hung parliament.	The Liberal Democrats only increased their share of the vote by 1% in 2010 and lost seats in the election compared to 2005. Therefore, strong debate performances perhaps do not matter as much as people think.
In 2015, Ed Miliband fell off the stage in front of a live television audience, which did little to enhance his image as a strong leader.	Miliband gave a better than expected performance when interviewed on TV by Jeremy Paxman during the 2015 election campaign, yet still lost the election.
Theresa May's refusal to participate in a live TV debate became a means of attacking her leadership. Green Party leader Caroline Lucas MP, who did take part in the debate, said that 'The first rule of leadership is that you show up.'	The debates between Johnson and Corbyn in 2019 were largely seen as dull and repetitive without an obvious winner.

> **Now test yourself**
>
> 13 Give two examples of how television appearances may have affected an election outcome.
>
> 14 Give two examples of how television appearances may have not affected an election outcome.
>
> **Answers online**
>
> TESTED

The role of social media

As a relatively recent innovation, it is only possible to consider the role of social media (YouTube, Facebook, Twitter, Instagram and other social media platforms) in the last decade of elections. The arguments and examples contained in Table 4.18 help us to consider the impact that social media have had upon election campaigns.

Table 4.18 Social media and general election outcomes

Influence of social media	Limits to influence
+ Labour's use of viral videos in 2017, shared among young Facebook users at minimal cost, demonstrated how the party could circumvent traditional print and broadcast media to spread its message. + UKIP had begun to reach out to voters on Facebook in 2015 and spent much of its campaign money on a social media campaign. This helped it win 3.8 million votes at the 2015 general election. + The winter general election of 2019 meant social media played a more important role than traditional canvassing, such as knocking on doors, due to adverse weather.	+ There have been many false dawns. The 'Webcameron' YouTube channel in 2010 was branded nothing more than a publicity stunt. + The Conservatives halved their spending on Facebook election adverts in 2019. + Use of social media is unlikely to win over new voters but rather 'preach to the converted', as the content consumed by users largely affirms their own views. In this sense, social media simply act as an echo chamber.

> **Canvassing** A form of campaigning that involve direct contact with voters. It includes political parties identifying supporters and undecided voters, persuasion through one-to-one conversations and efforts to 'get out the vote'.

> **Remember**
>
> It is easy to discount the role of print media given the growth of social media. Yet many of the major newspapers have a substantial online presence.

Case studies of three general elections

Results

+ The Conservative Party won a 43-seat majority.
+ Labour lost 62 seats.
+ The House of Commons was dominated by Labour and the Conservatives, with little representation for smaller parties.
+ Margaret Thatcher became the first female prime minister.
+ This marked the beginning of 18 consecutive years of Conservative government.

Social factors

+ The growing size of the middle class and shrinking working class gave the Conservatives a natural advantage.
+ Thatcher's attempt to become the 'housewives' friend', with a focus on food prices, may have tempted more women to vote Conservative.
+ The Conservatives managed to win 41% of the C2 vote, up from 21% in 1974.

Valence issues

+ Governing competency: there had been a wave of public-sector strikes in 1978–79. Voters punished Labour for not controlling trade union power.
+ Economic competence: Labour became associated with high inflation.
+ Party unity: Labour was beginning to appear disunited between its left wing and its moderates.

Salient issues

+ The extent to which the state should regulate and control industry became a key issue.
+ The Conservative promise to expand home ownership was popular.

The election campaign

+ Labour ran a poor election campaign, implying that the country should not elect a woman.
+ In contrast, the Conservatives responded with a slick, media-driven campaign that involved hiring the Saatchi Brothers. This advertising agency developed the 'Labour isn't working' advertising campaign.

Media influence

+ The *Sun* switched allegiance from Labour to Conservative and ran the damning headline of 'Crisis, what crisis?' when reporting on Labour leader James Callaghan's supposed blasé attitude towards the industrial unrest.

> **Exam tip**
>
> Instead of giving descriptive details of a specific election, evaluate the different factors (social factors, valence issues etc.) by deciding which ones best explain voting behaviour. In 1979 it is likely that valence issues following the 'winter of discontent' played the most important role. Opinion polls showed that Labour might have won if it had called the election in 1978, before the wave of strikes had hit the country.

Results

+ Labour won a landslide victory, culminating in 419 seats and a 187-seat majority.
+ The Conservatives lost 178 seats and recorded their worst election result since 1906.
+ The Liberal Democrats made a breakthrough, winning 46 seats at Westminster.
+ The effects of the electoral system exaggerated the scale of Labour's victory — 43% of the vote was converted into 63% of the seats.

Social factors

+ Labour won more votes than the Conservatives in nearly every demographic group and so it is difficult to see a particular social factor that stood out.
+ However, Blair was able to appeal to the growing middle class with his 'Third Way' policies.
+ Labour also won back the C2 skilled manual workers who had abandoned the party from 1979 onwards.

→

Answers and quick quizzes at **www.hoddereducation.co.uk/myrevisionnotesdownloads**

Valence issues

+ Governing competency: the Tories had been mired in a number of scandals, including the 'arms to Iraq' affair and the 'cash for questions' scandal.
+ Economic competence: Labour had worked hard to regain trust, promising to stick to Tory spending plans and not to raise income tax.
+ Party unity: Conservative prime minister John Major had faced a leadership contest in 1995 and the party was bitterly divided over Europe.
+ Party leaders: Blair was seen as a charismatic, dynamic leader while John Major, the Conservative prime minister, was viewed as dull and uninspiring.

Salient issues

+ Public services took centre stage. Labour promised to invest in education and health, and to be 'tough on crime, tough on the causes of crime'.

The election campaign

+ Tory attempts to paint Blair as a socialist backfired with the 'New Labour, New Danger' campaign.
+ While opinion polls narrowed towards the end, the lengthy campaign appeared to have little impact upon the trajectory of the result.

Media influence

+ The Murdoch press switched support from Conservative to Labour. The *Sun* ran with the headline 'The Sun backs Blair'.

Now test yourself

15 Give three reasons why valence issues appeared to be particularly important in deciding the outcome of the 1997 general election.

16 List two things that benefited Labour in 1997 that they didn't benefit from in 1979.

Answers online

TESTED ◯

Case study: the 2019 general election

Results

+ The Conservatives won an 80-seat majority, ending 2 years of minority government.
+ Labour was reduced to just 203 seats, its worst defeat since 1935.
+ The Liberal Democrats' hoped-for comeback failed to materialise, with the party winning 11 seats, one fewer than in 2017.
+ The SNP dominated in Scotland, winning 48 out of 59 Scottish seats and comfortably remaining the third largest party in the House of Commons.

Social factors

+ Regional divides appeared to play an important role in deciding the election.
+ The Conservatives were able to breach Labour's 'red wall', winning seats in the North and Midlands that had been considered safe for generations.
+ The Tories benefited from consolidating the Leave vote in areas that had voted heavily to leave the EU in the 2016 referendum. Labour failed to do a similar thing in Remain-voting areas.
+ Similarly to 2017, age again emerged as the clearest indicator of voting behaviour, with 56% of 18–24-year-olds voting Labour and 57% of 60–69-year-olds voting Conservative.

Valence issues

+ Party unity: by removing the whip (see Chapter 6) from Tory MPs who voted to block a no-deal Brexit, Boris Johnson went into the general election campaign with party candidates who were united by his approach to leaving the EU.
+ Economic competence: opinion polls showed that voters still did not trust Labour on the economy, particularly its spending plans.

+ Party leaders: Corbyn's failure to tackle anti-Semitism in his party played a significant role in weakening his approval ratings.

Salient issues

+ The Tory promise to 'get Brexit done' appealed to a public weary of three-and-a-half years of political gridlock in Parliament, unlike the Labour promise for another referendum.
+ Healthcare spending also appeared to be important to voters. All the main parties promised increases in health spending. The Tories sought to defuse criticism of public-sector cuts by promising 50,000 extra nurses, even if they later had to admit that only 31,000 of those would be new recruits.

The election campaign

+ The Brexit Party's decision not to field candidates against Leave-supporting Conservative MPs helped to consolidate the Leave vote for the Tories, which proved crucial in marginal constituencies.
+ The Conservatives played it safe with their electoral promises, while Labour's promise of free broadband for all was met with cynicism.
+ Johnson ran a traditional campaign with a number of high-profile media events, including one where he smashed through a wall labelled 'Gridlock', driving a JCB emblazoned with 'Get Brexit Done' on the front. Repetitive sloganeering appeared to work.

Media influence

+ Negative coverage of Jeremy Corbyn continued in the press, similarly to 2017.
+ Yet the Conservatives had caught up with Labour when it came to effective use of social media. They targeted older voters on Facebook in marginal constituencies with adverts about Brexit.

Exam practice

1 Evaluate the view that the media play a crucial part in determining the outcome of elections in the UK. [30]

2 Evaluate the view that election campaigns and party manifestos influence the outcome of general elections. [30]

3 Using the source, evaluate the view that party leaders play the most important role in determining how people vote in elections. [30]

The one constant in recent elections has been the relentless focus upon party leaders in election campaigns. Do they appear decisive and 'prime ministerial'? Are they in command of their party, do they look comfortable in front of a live television audience and do they sound ordinary? These are the sorts of questions that go through the minds of voters. If the connection between the electorate and the leader is lacking, it is unlikely a party will win. Rather than compare party manifestos, voters compare leaders. This point was highlighted in 2019 with Johnson and the deeply unpopular Corbyn. It was also true in 1997 with voters preferring the charismatic Blair instead of the grey, dull figure of John Major.

However, while it is unlikely a party will win with an unpopular leader, it is also not a foregone conclusion. Corbyn managed to improve Labour's vote share despite his unpopularity in 2017, while Thatcher was never as popular as her ardent followers might have you believe. There are other factors that come into play. Trust in a party's economic promises is every bit as important as trust in its leader. There may well be a salient issue that is decisive. Also, demographic changes can shift the voting patterns of an important section of the electorate.

Source: original material

In your response you must:
+ compare and contrast the different opinions in the source
+ examine and debate these views in a balanced way
+ analyse and evaluate only the information presented in the source

Answers and quick quiz 4 online

Exam skills

In a source question, first decide whether you agree with the statement in the question. Then try to pair up an argument that supports your view and a counter-argument that doesn't, but which shares a similar theme or common thread. This exercise is performed in the table below for question 3 in the Exam practice box.

Source argument	Source counter-argument
'If the connection between the electorate and the leader is lacking, it is unlikely a party will win.'	'While it is unlikely a party will win with an unpopular leader, it is also not a foregone conclusion.'
'Rather than compare party manifestos, voters compare leaders.'	'Trust in a party's economic promises is every bit as important as trust in its leader.'
'This point was highlighted in 2019 with Johnson and the deeply unpopular Corbyn.'	'Corbyn managed to improve Labour's vote share despite his unpopularity in 2017.'

Summary

You should now have an understanding of:
+ the influence of social class on voting behaviour
+ the influence of other demographic factors such as age, region, gender and ethnicity
+ the role that valence issues play in electoral outcomes
+ the role that party leaders play in affecting how people vote
+ how salient issues may affect voting behaviour
+ the debates about turnout and tactical voting, and whether these affect electoral outcomes
+ debates about the significance of general election campaigns, specifically party manifestos
+ the debates around the use and impact of opinion polls
+ the significance of different forms of media in affecting election outcomes

5 The constitution

What is a constitution?

A constitution in politics can be described as a set of rules which regulates the system of government and politics of a country. It has the following functions:
+ It establishes the distribution of power within the state.
+ In so doing, it also establishes the relationships between the institutions that make up the state.
+ It establishes the limits of government power.
+ It asserts the rights of the citizens and how these may be protected.
+ It describes how the constitution itself can be amended — what the procedure is for such a process.

> **Constitution** A set of rules that establishes a country's governmental and political system.

The development of the UK Constitution

The UK Constitution has developed over many centuries. The reasons for its slow, gradual development are twofold:
1 It is known as an organic constitution that has been shaped by gradual changes in UK society and politics. It has never been imposed on the UK at a single event.
2 There has never been a historical event, such as a revolution, which has overturned the existing order and therefore heralded in a new political order. In the civil war and Commonwealth period of 1642–60, the monarchy was replaced by parliamentary government and later by dictatorship (of Oliver Cromwell). All attempts to write a constitution failed, so monarchy was restored.

> **Organic constitution** A political constitution that has developed naturally in accordance with changes in the nature of society and the political system, as opposed to a constitution which is created at one historical moment in time.

Table 5.1 shows the main stages in the development of the UK Constitution.

Table 5.1 Stages in the development of the UK Constitution

Historical event	Description
Magna Carta, 1215	An agreement between the nobles and the king. It established the principle of the rule of law, i.e. that government must operate within the law and the law should apply equally to all citizens.
Bill of Rights, 1689	An agreement between the king and Parliament. It established the idea of the sovereignty of Parliament over the king in matters of legislation.
Act of Settlement, 1701	Established the monarch's position as ruler of England, Scotland, Wales and Ireland. It also established that the rules of succession to the throne should be determined by Parliament.
Act of Union, 1707	Dissolved the Scottish Parliament and established the union of Great Britain and Ireland.
Parliament Acts, 1911 and 1949	Limited the power of the House of Lords to delaying legislation for one year and took away the house's power over financial matters.
European Communities Act, 1972	Established the UK's entry into the European Community (EU).
European Union (Withdrawal Agreement) Act 2020	Confirmed the UK's decision to leave the EU following the EU referendum in 2016.

Now test yourself

TESTED ◯

1 Describe three functions of a constitution.
2 Why might the UK Constitution be described as 'organic'?
3 Explain three recent stages of development of the UK Constitution.

Answers online

71

The nature and principles of the UK Constitution

The UK has an uncodified constitution:

✚ The UK Constitution is not written down in one single document.
✚ It can be found in multiple places, including in statute law (acts of Parliament), conventions (unwritten rules that have the force of law) and historical texts (such as the Magna Carta).
✚ The UK Constitution is therefore multi-sourced.
✚ The UK is unlike most other countries, which tend to have codified constitutions, such as the USA and France.

> **Uncodified constitution** A constitution that is not contained in a single document and has a number of different sources.
>
> **Codified constitution** A constitution that can be found in one single document and so has one single source. Constitutional laws are seen as superior to ordinary laws and have a separate amendment procedure.

> **Remember**
>
> The UK Constitution is uncodified but this does not mean it is 'unwritten', as some commentators have described it. Much of the UK Constitution *is* written down. For example, all acts of Parliament are written. All the word 'uncodified' means is that the constitution is not contained in a single document.

The UK Constitution is unentrenched:

✚ Any part of the UK Constitution can be changed with a single act of Parliament.
✚ For example, the Human Rights Act could be scrapped or amended if Parliament passed a law to do so.
✚ The UK is unlike most other countries, which tend to have entrenched constitutions.
✚ A constitution that is entrenched is protected from short-term amendment.
✚ For example, the US Constitution requires a complicated procedure whereby three-quarters of the 50 states and two-thirds of both houses of Congress must agree to change the constitution.
✚ Uncodified constitutions are therefore easier to change. For better or worse, they are more flexible.

> **Unentrenched constitution** A constitution that can be amended by an individual government or parliament.
>
> **Entrenched constitution** A constitution that has special arrangements to safeguard it from being amended by a temporary government or legislature. Entrenchment is closely associated with codified constitutions.

> **Remember**
>
> You should not separate the concepts of a codified and an entrenched constitution. If the UK were to adopt a codified constitution, it would also have to be entrenched. If it were not entrenched, codifying the constitution would be futile as it could be changed by any future Parliament.

The UK Parliament is sovereign:

✚ Parliamentary sovereignty means that Parliament is the supreme decision-making body in the UK. It is legally sovereign.
✚ Any decision made elsewhere in the UK can be overturned by an act of Parliament.
✚ No Parliament is bound by previous decisions.
✚ This is why the Labour government was able to devolve power to London after the Thatcher government had abolished the Greater London Council.
✚ No Parliament can bind future Parliaments.
✚ For this reason, the Conservative Party can scrap the Fixed-term Parliaments Act, as promised in its 2019 general election manifesto.

> **Parliamentary sovereignty** The concept that Parliament is the supreme decision-making body in the UK.

Answers and quick quizzes at **www.hoddereducation.co.uk/myrevisionnotesdownloads**

There are many different forms of sovereignty, which are described in Table 5.2.

Table 5.2 Different forms of sovereignty

Form of sovereignty	Description
Legal sovereignty	Legal sovereignty refers to formal power, which usually lies where laws are made. In the UK, Parliament is seen to have legal sovereignty.
Political sovereignty	This refers to the body, institution or group that *in practice* holds the most influence over decision making. In the UK, the governing party, the cabinet and the prime minister are often thought of as having political sovereignty, in part due to their dominance over Parliament.
Popular sovereignty	Popular sovereignty rests with the electorate, which votes in referendums and elections, the outcomes of which are *in practice* binding on Parliament.
Devolved sovereignty	Parliament agrees for other bodies or institutions to take decisions. These 'devolved' powers can be taken back by the UK Parliament at a later date.

The rule of law is applied. A. V. Dicey (1885) wrote that the rule of law consists of three strands:

1 No one can be punished without trial.
2 No individual or institution is considered above the law, including the government, which means that all citizens are subject to the same justice.
3 An independent judiciary can hold government ministers to account, and this judiciary ought to be free from governmental interference. In practice this means that citizens can take the government to court, and that the government must act in accordance with the law, not making arbitrary rules.

> **Rule of law** The principle that equal justice should apply to all. This by extension requires the government to follow the law as laid down by parliament.

In the UK, it is expected that the government must follow the law as set out by acts of Parliament.

Now test yourself   TESTED ○

4 Complete the table below by defining the key terms.

Key term	Explanation
Uncodified constitution	
Unentrenched constitution	
Parliamentary sovereignty	

5 Describe the difference between legal and political sovereignty.

Answers online

> **Unitary constitution** A constitution which establishes that legal sovereignty resides in one location. Under a unitary constitution, power can be delegated to subsidiary bodies, but this power can be returned to the sovereign body.
>
> **Federal constitution** A constitution where legal sovereignty is divided between the central government and regional governments. The powers of the regional bodies are protected by an entrenched constitution.

The UK has a unitary constitution:

+ In the UK, ultimate political power rests in one geographical location — Westminster.
+ All the important political institutions are located here, including Parliament, government departments and the UK Supreme Court.
+ These institutions have power and authority over every other decision-making body, such as devolved parliaments and local councils.
+ This point was confirmed by the UK Supreme Court in 2017 when it ruled that only the UK Parliament, and not the devolved bodies, could confirm or deny Britain's withdrawal from the EU.
+ In having a unitary constitution the UK differs from other countries, such as the USA, which have federal constitutions.
+ Under a federal constitution, the division of powers reserved to regional bodies is symmetrical — that is, they all have equal powers.

73

There is a fusion of powers between the government and Parliament in the UK:

+ The fusion of powers is associated with a parliamentary system of government and is another key principle of the UK Constitution.
+ The government is drawn from the legislature, which is to say that members of the government must also be MPs or peers.
+ For example, the prime minister is also an MP. All members of the UK cabinet are either MPs or peers.
+ The highest court of appeal, formerly known as the Law Lords, also convened in Parliament, until the recent creation of the UK Supreme Court.
+ The fusion of powers contrasts sharply with the separation of powers that is common in presidential systems of government.
+ In these systems, the executive (government), legislature (parliament) and judiciary (courts) are separate from one another and are staffed by separate personnel.

> **Fusion of powers** The government is made up of individuals who are members of either the House of Commons or the House of Lords.
>
> **Separation of powers** The powers of the different branches of government are clearly defined and separated, as are the personnel.

Now test yourself　　　　　　　　　　　　　TESTED ◯

6　Describe the difference between fusion of powers and separation of powers.

7　Why is the UK Constitution described as unitary?

Answers online

How have the constitutional principles changed?

As will be discussed later in this chapter, constitutional reform has reshaped much of the UK's Constitution. Table 5.3 describes how some of the principles of the UK Constitution have been affected by these developments.

Table 5.3 How the UK constitutional principles have changed over time

Principle	How this principle has been affected by constitutional reform
Uncodified	The UK Constitution remains uncodified but can perhaps be found in fewer sources. + For example, the UK's withdrawal from the EU will remove an important source of law. In addition, an increasing number of previously unwritten sources of the Constitution are being written into statute law. + For example, the Human Rights Act wrote the European Convention of Human Rights into UK law.
Unentrenched	Parts of the UK Constitution are effectively becoming semi-entrenched. + Governments have sought to informally entrench their policies through referendums. + The Scottish Parliament is safe from abolition because Scottish voters decided overwhelmingly in favour of devolution.
Parliament is sovereign	Popular sovereignty has increasingly come into conflict with parliamentary sovereignty as a result of referendums. + The outcome of the EU referendum in 2016 was not legally binding on Parliament, but *in practice* resulted in the passing of the EU (Withdrawal Agreement) Act 2020.
Unitary	As a result of devolution, it is now possible to describe the UK Constitution as 'quasi-federal' (semi-federal). + Different laws exist in different parts of the country. + The UK Constitution is neither as unitary as it once was, nor can it be described as federal, since devolution has occurred at a different pace across the country and the powers of devolved bodies vary considerably from region to region.
Fusion of powers	The Law Lords used to be the highest court in the land and held court cases in the House of Lords. Now, the UK Supreme Court convenes in a different building altogether, and thus there is greater separation of powers in relation to the judiciary.

Remember

It is useful to distinguish constitutional principles which exist in theory (*de jure*) and those which exist in practice (de facto). Devolution could be scrapped by the UK Parliament *de jure* but not de facto since the devolved bodies were approved of by the people in referendums.

Exam tip

When answering a question, it is important not only to identify an argument but also to *explain* its relevance to the question. A useful sentence starter is 'This point is relevant to the question because...'. Let's imagine that the exam question is 'Evaluate the view that the principles of the UK Constitution have changed beyond recognition.' If you write about semi-entrenchment, you could write the following:

This point is relevant to the question because it shows that it is becoming more difficult to change the Constitution than it was before, as in practice a decision made through a referendum will likely require a subsequent referendum to change it, instead of a simple act of Parliament.

The sources of the UK Constitution

Because the UK Constitution is not codified, it has several different sources. Table 5.4 shows these sources, with examples.

Table 5.4 The sources of the UK Constitution

Source	Description	Examples
Statute law	Laws passed by Parliament	Human Rights Act 1998 Constitutional Reform Act 2005
Constitutional **conventions**	Unwritten rules which are considered to be binding on all members of the political community	Salisbury Convention Collective cabinet responsibility
Foreign **treaties** and agreements	Agreements with external bodies that bind the UK in some way	European Convention on Human Rights with the Council of Europe
Authoritative works	The writings of constitutional experts that clarify the meaning of the Constitution	A. V. Dicey's *Law of the Constitution*, 1885 Walter Bagehot's *The English Constitution*, 1867
Common law and tradition	Rules that have been passed down through various judgments in court cases	The rules of parliamentary procedure and discipline Various rights such as freedom of expression

Statute law Any law that has been passed by the UK Parliament and has received royal assent.

Conventions Unwritten political rules or practices that are considered binding, such as the Salisbury Convention that prevents the House of Lords from blocking manifesto proposals.

Treaties Agreements with external bodies that bind the UK in some way.

Authoritative works Historical books and documents that clarify the meaning of constitutional principles.

Common law Unwritten laws that have not been passed by Parliament but have passed down through history in the form of judicial precedents.

Now test yourself

TESTED

8 Look at these sources of the UK Constitution. In each case, identify one example.

Constitutional source	Example
Parliamentary statute	
Work of authority	
Constitutional convention	
Common law and tradition	
External treaty or agreement	

Answers online

Constitutional reform, 1997–2010

The purposes of constitutional reform in this period were to address the following shortcomings:
+ The political system needed to be more democratic.
+ The political system was too centralised, with too much power in too few hands.
+ Citizens' rights were inadequately protected.
+ The political system needed to be modernised and brought into line with other modern democracies.

The reforms during this period included devolution, the introduction of the Human Rights Act, House of Lords reform, the Freedom of Information Act and the creation of the UK Supreme Court

Devolution

REVISED

Devolution during this period involved the transfer of extensive powers away from Westminster and Whitehall to governments and elected assemblies in Scotland, Wales and Northern Ireland. A Greater London Authority was also created along with the office of London Mayor.

Devolution in the UK has the following features:
+ It is the transfer of powers but not sovereignty to the three national regions of the UK.
+ Originally the funding for devolved services came from a central government annual grant, but increasingly the devolved governments have gained independent control over taxes raised in their countries.
+ The size of the devolution grants has been calculated using the 'Barnett formula', which takes account of the fact that the three countries have greater needs than England.
+ It is asymmetric, meaning that the three regions have not been granted the same powers.
+ The devolved administrations each have an elected assembly (parliament in Scotland and Wales) and an executive, or government, which is drawn from the assembly.
+ The method of election of the assemblies is not first-past-the-post but by forms of proportional representation.
+ In general, devolution has been entrenched by referendums.
+ The UK Parliament has the option of bringing back the powers to Westminster and has suspended devolved government in Northern Ireland several times.

> **Devolution** A process whereby power, but not legal sovereignty, is distributed away from central government to regional governments.
>
> **Asymmetric devolution** The situation where the extent of powers that are transferred from Westminster differ from one place to another.

The powers of the devolved bodies

Table 5.5 lists the powers of the Scottish Parliament, Welsh Parliament and Northern Irish Assembly, including powers of specific taxes.

Table 5.5 The powers of the devolved bodies

Policy area	Scotland	Wales	Northern Ireland
Education	✓	✓	✓
Housing	✓	✓	✓
Environment	✓	✓	✓
Health and social care	✓	✓	✓
Culture and sport	✓	✓	✓
Justice and policing	✓	✗	✓
Social security and employment	✓	✗	✓
Transport	✓	✓	✓
Business	✓	✓	✓
Energy	✗	✗	✓
Taxes	**Scotland**	**Wales**	**Northern Ireland**
Local property tax	✓	✓	✓
Stamp duty	✓	✓	✗
Landfill tax	✓	✓	✗
Income tax	✓	✓	✗
Air passenger duty	✓	✗	✓
Revenue from VAT	✓	✗	✗
Corporation tax	✗	✗	✓

Source: Institute for Government

Now test yourself   TESTED ◯

9 Look at these powers. Which countries of the UK, not including England, have these powers?

Power	Countries
Justice and policing	
Income tax levels	
Education	

Answers online

Table 5.6 considers the debate regarding the impact of devolution.

Table 5.6 Positive and negative impact of devolution

Positive aspects	Negative aspects
Devolution makes government much more region-sensitive: the devolved bodies deliver different policy from that produced by Westminster.	Devolution has created the perception of regional unfairness. For example, all Welsh people under the age of 25 can receive free prescriptions while not all can in England.
Power sharing in Northern Ireland has significantly reduced sectarian violence.	There is uncertainty over whether non-English MPs in Westminster should be voting on issues only relevant to England.
The electoral systems used to elect the devolved bodies (AMS and STV) are more proportional, and thus create greater legitimacy and prevent single-party domination.	The nature of these electoral systems makes power sharing between different political parties more likely, which in turn can lead to less stable governments. In 2017 the coalition between Sinn Fein and the DUP collapsed, and neither won enough seats under STV to choose another coalition partner.

Human Rights Act (HRA) 1998

REVISED

This act brought the European Convention on Human Rights (ECHR) into UK law. It is binding on all bodies except the UK Parliament. Table 5.7 considers the debate about the impact of the Human Rights Act.

Table 5.7 The positive and negative impact of the Human Rights Act

Positive aspects	Negative aspects
It allowed UK citizens to appeal to UK courts instead of going abroad to fight for their rights in the European Court of Human Rights in Strasbourg, making access to justice more affordable and accessible to UK citizens.	Conservatives believe that the Human Rights Act has given unelected judges too much power over the elected government.
The Act strikes the right balance between those who are concerned with parliamentary sovereignty (Parliament can amend the Human Rights Act if it wishes to) and those who wish to hold Parliament to a high standard (the Act forces Parliament to take account of the ECHR when passing law).	Many liberal commentators believe that the HRA is not strong enough, pointing to a lack of entrenchment. The HRA can be weakened or scrapped with a simple act of Parliament, a prospect made more likely with the Conservatives' 80-seat majority.
The Act also limits the power of the government because of the ability of the Supreme Court to issue incompatibility statements, which direct government to think again on legislation that appears to conflict with the HRA.	Parliament, and by extension the government, can ignore incompatibility statements.

House of Lords reform

REVISED

+ All but 93 of the hereditary peers (those members of the House of Lords who could pass on their position to family members) were removed. The Act reduced the House of Lords' membership from 1,330 to 669 mainly life peers.
+ Only life peers can now be appointed to the Lords.
+ All Lords appointments are now made by an independent commission instead of the prime minister.

Table 5.8 considers whether House of Lords reform has had a positive impact.

Table 5.8 The positive and negative impact of Labour's House of Lords reform

Positive aspects	Negative aspects
The most undemocratic element of the House of Lords has largely been removed — the hereditary principle.	The reforms were supposed to be the first stage of a two-stage process, which would eventually lead to a partly or fully elected chamber. This second stage has not happened.
By abolishing most of the hereditary peers, Labour in effect ended the inbuilt Conservative majority in the chamber, which would mean that future Conservative governments would be scrutinised more effectively.	The Lords doesn't have enough power to hold the government to account as it is constrained by the Salisbury Convention (it can't block manifesto items) and by the Parliament Acts (it can only delay for one year and has no say over budgets).
The creation of an independent body to approve appointments limits the potential for a government to pack the Lords with its own supporters.	In reality, party leaders and specifically the prime minister remain influential when it comes to the awarding of peerages, which is a useful way of rewarding supporters.

Freedom of Information Act (FOI) 2000

REVISED

This law granted the legal right to individuals and organisations to access official information held by all public bodies, except for information concerning national security. Table 5.9 considers the debate regarding the success of the Freedom of Information Act.

Table 5.9 The positive and negative impact of the Freedom of Information Act

Positive aspects	Negative aspects
Prior to the Act, Labour criticised the Tories for 'excessive secrecy' and so introduced the Act in order to create more opportunities for scrutiny of the government in the wake of scandals such as those over 'mad cow disease' (BSE) and 'arms to Iraq'.	The law has not prevented further cover-ups. For example, journalists hoping to get access to MPs' expense claims through an FOI request found that the information released to them was heavily redacted, which led to information being acquired through leaks instead.
The law brought the UK into line with other Western democracies, such as the USA, which had similar FOI laws.	It is far weaker than similar laws in other countries. For example, the security services were exempted, MPs exempted their own correspondence with each other, and arms deals were also exempted.
The Act has allowed the public to understand more about how government works and the relationship between government departments, the prime minister and so on — even interactions between the royal family and politicians. The so-called 'black spider memos' were released using a FOI request, which revealed how Prince Charles was privately criticising government policy.	The government has scope to limit the law still further. For instance, after the release of the 'black spider memos', the government amended the FOI Act to exempt royal correspondence.

The creation of the UK Supreme Court

REVISED

+ The Constitutional Reform Act 2005 took the 12 most senior judges out of the House of Lords and created instead the UK Supreme Court, the highest court of appeal and legal interpretation in the country.
+ It also guaranteed the independence of the judiciary, taking the appointment of judges out of political hands, and replaced the lord chancellor, a cabinet minister, as head of the judiciary by the lord chief justice, a senior judge.

Table 5.10 outlines the debate about whether the creation of the UK Supreme Court has been successful.

Table 5.10 The UK Supreme Court: has it been a success?

Positive aspects	Negative aspects
As a separate institution from Parliament, the UK Supreme Court enjoys greater independence and is willing to challenge the government, as demonstrated when the court prevented Boris Johnson from proroguing Parliament for political reasons in September 2019.	The Supreme Court does not have much more power than the body it replaced. It can only interpret laws passed by Parliament, whereas courts in European countries and in the USA can strike down laws that are deemed unconstitutional. The Supreme Court is only allowed as much power as it is given by Parliament, and the power it currently has can be taken away. The Conservatives pledged to review the extent of the Supreme Court's powers in their 2019 election manifesto, which may affect how well it can hold the government to account.
Senior judges are appointed by the Judicial Appointments Commission, reducing the possibility of political interference in the selection of judges and increasing the likelihood that the Supreme Court would act without bias by simply applying the law.	Some on the left accuse the court of having a conservative bias, owing to the justices' narrow social background. Others on the right believe that the court has used its position to enter into the political arena. They point to the 2017 Miller case, which denied the government the ability to trigger Article 50, a mechanism notifying the EU of the UK's intention to leave, without first seeking approval from Parliament.

Now test yourself — TESTED

10 Complete the table below by filling in the gaps.

Reform	What it involved
Devolution	Concerned the _____ of power from Westminster to regional bodies
Human Rights Act	Wrote the _____ into UK law
House of Lords reform	Removed most of the _____ from the House of Lords
Freedom of Information Act	Allowed citizens and investigative journalists access to information deemed to be in the _____
Creation of the UK Supreme Court	Replaced the _____ and moved the UK's top court out of the House of _____

Answers online

Constitutional reform, 2010 to present

The objectives of constitutional reform since 2010 have been:
+ to decentralise power away from London and central government
+ to increase political stability by fixing election dates
+ to increase MPs' accountability to voters
+ to address the so-called 'West Lothian question'
+ to guarantee the UK's withdrawal from the EU in accordance with the result of the 2016 referendum

The coalition government between 2010 and 2015 was committed to some reforms, largely under the influence of the Liberal Democrats, who shared power with the Conservatives. These included the Fixed-term Parliaments Act 2011 and the Recall of MPs Act 2015. Yet the restoration of single-party government since 2015 has not limited the pace of constitutional reform.

During this period, the Conservatives have supported further devolution measures: English Votes for English Laws (EVEL) and, perhaps the most significant of all reforms, the EU Withdrawal Act 2020. These reforms are explained and analysed in more detail below.

Fixed-term Parliaments Act 2011

REVISED

+ The dates of general elections were taken out of the control of the prime minister.
+ Elections were to take place every 5 years.
+ An early election can be called if approved by a two-thirds majority of the House of Commons, or if the government loses a vote of no confidence.
+ Furthermore, a vote of no confidence in a government could not be tied to an ordinary piece of legislation but instead had to be dealt with as a separate motion in the House of Commons.

Table 5.11 considers arguments in favour of and against the Fixed-term Parliaments Act 2011.

Table 5.11 The strengths and weaknesses of the Fixed-term Parliaments Act 2011

Strengths	Weaknesses
This Act aims to reduce the power of the prime minister. Prime ministers can no longer call a snap election on their own to capitalise on a favourable moment in time for the governing party, as Thatcher did to benefit from her popularity after the Falklands War.	It could allow an unpopular government to continue in office for a full 5-year term, so it may not necessarily weaken the power of government. Due to parliamentary sovereignty, it is possible for this Act to be amended, replaced or even scrapped, as the Conservative Party pledged in its 2019 election manifesto.
Governments can no longer tie a vote on an ordinary piece of legislation to a vote of no confidence in order to quell backbench dissent in their own party (as John Major's government did for the Maastricht Treaty). As a result, the new rule means that MPs may feel more inclined to vote with their conscience on important issues.	Governments can still manipulate outcomes to suit them. For example, they might alter policies in such a way that voters feel a positive impact (perhaps through cuts to income tax) just before election time, which is easier to do when the election date is fixed.
The Act is intended to ensure greater political stability, which was particularly important during the coalition years, where either the Conservatives or the Liberal Democrats might have otherwise withdrawn from government at any moment.	The law has not prevented snap elections from being called. Theresa May broke the spirit of the law in 2017 by asking Parliament to vote for an election. In 2019 a snap winter election was again called. On both occasions, the governing party wished to capitalise on their advantage in the opinion polls.

> **Exam tip**
>
> When you include an argument and a counter-argument in a paragraph, it is important to be clear when the first argument ends and the counter-argument starts. The word 'However' is a useful connective (as are 'Yet' and 'On the other hand') to help you do this.

Further devolution

REVISED

The government focused upon extending powers to the existing devolved bodies, particularly in Scotland and in Wales. It also introduced some new devolved authorities in England.

Scotland

+ The Scotland Act 2016 increased the devolved powers of the Scottish government and Parliament.
+ These powers centred upon welfare provision and the payment levels for some social security benefits.

81

+ It also granted power to set the rates of income tax in Scotland and to determine how the receipts from income tax should be spent.
+ In addition, the Scottish government gained control over half the proceeds of VAT raised in Scotland.
+ The Act made devolution effectively permanent by accepting that its removal could only occur via a future referendum.

Wales

+ The Wales Act 2014 gave the Welsh government limited powers to raise new forms of tax and to control the revenue from them.
+ In 2015 the UK government allowed the Welsh Assembly to claim control over income tax revenue raised in Wales.
+ The Wales Act 2017 allowed the Welsh Assembly to determine its own electoral system (though not for general elections).
+ It allowed the Welsh Assembly to turn itself into a parliament, giving it limited law-making functions.
+ Wales also gained increased power over public services.

The election of mayors in cities and regions

+ From 2017 onwards, six cities and regions elected mayors with varying degrees of independent power, such as over planning, transport, housing and policing.
+ The most prominent region was the Greater Manchester Combined Authority.

The impact of further devolution

Table 5.12 considers the debate around the impact of further devolution since 2010.

Table 5.12 The positive and negative impact of further devolution since 2010

Positive impact	Negative impact
In Scotland, it was hoped that increasing the power of the Scottish Parliament would limit the appeal of Scottish independence. Those who take this view argue that Scotland now has the most powerful sub-national government in Europe.	Scottish nationalists still believe that the additional powers granted to Scotland following the Scottish independence referendum in 2014 do not go far enough. They say that Scotland should have complete control over setting its own interest rates.
In Wales, devolution has been more evolutionary in nature, as support for the creation of the Welsh Assembly was initially limited. However, over time Wales has been granted more power in line with increased support for the devolved arrangements.	The powers of the devolved bodies are still subject to approval by Westminster. For example, despite demands to devolve policing and justice to Wales, the UK government declined.
The newly elected mayors in England have ensured better representation for their regions and cities. For example, the mayor of Greater Manchester, Andy Burnham, drew attention to the lack of consultation with regional authorities by the government during the Covid-19 pandemic.	Critics argue that these mayors have received limited powers. In October 2020, Greater Manchester was placed into a higher tier of lockdown restrictions regardless of what its mayor had called for. Large parts of England remain highly centralised.

Now test yourself   TESTED

11 Describe two new powers that the devolved authorities in Scotland have gained since 2010.
12 Describe two new powers that the devolved authorities in Wales have gained since 2010.

Answers online

Recall of MPs Act 2015

This law gives constituents the power to order their MP to face a by-election if they have been found guilty of serious misconduct. The process of recalling an MP is illustrated in Figure 5.1.

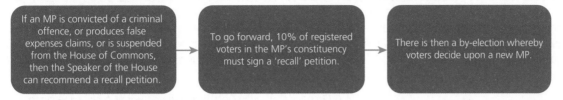

Figure 5.1 How a recall election is triggered

Table 5.13 considers the impact, both positive and negative, of the Recall of MPs Act 2015.

Table 5.13 The positive and negative impact of the Recall of MPs Act 2015

Positive aspects	Negative aspects
The Act aims to punish illegal or inappropriate actions while making it difficult to remove an MP for simply speaking their mind, therefore respecting the views of the electorate at the previous election.	A recall attempt does not guarantee that corruption or wrongdoing will be punished. Example: Despite his suspension from Parliament over his failure to declare hospitality received from the Sri Lankan government, Ian Paisley Jr did not have to face a by-election in his South Antrim constituency because the recall petition failed to garner enough signatures.
The Act is being used appropriately and as it was intended. Example: Labour MP Fiona Onasanya lost her seat after the Speaker agreed to trigger a recall petition in March 2019, following the rejection of her appeal against her conviction for perverting the course of justice.	The 'recalled' MP can still stand in the subsequent by-election. Example: Conservative MP Chris Davies stood in the Brecon and Radnorshire by-election in August 2019 despite being recalled after falsifying expenses claims.

Making links

The petition element of the recall procedure involves citizens in decision making — in this case the decision on whether to force a by-election. Therefore, recall elections can be seen as an important development in direct democracy. Tips on using synoptic links are given in the Exam skills box at the end of this chapter.

English Votes for English Laws (EVEL) 2015

+ A new parliamentary procedure was introduced whereby MPs representing Welsh, Scottish and Northern Ireland seats will not debate or vote on issues affecting only England (Figure 5.2).
+ It was an attempt to address the West Lothian question following devolution.
+ The new procedures were used for the first time in January 2016 when Scottish MPs were barred from voting on the Housing Bill.

> **West Lothian question**
> Refers to the dilemma posed by the devolution process, now that the UK Parliament addresses issues that are predominantly English in nature. It questions the involvement of non-English MPs in deciding these issues.

Figure 5.2 How EVEL works

Table 5.14 considers the debate about the impact, both positive and negative, of EVEL.

Table 5.14 The positive and negative aspects of EVEL

Positive aspects	Negative aspects
Proponents argue that it strikes the right balance by ensuring continued representation in Westminster for all UK citizens, while tackling the unfairness of the West Lothian question.	All MPs are still allowed a vote on the final reading of the bill, so in theory non-English MPs can still prevent a bill deemed English in nature from passing. Critics argue that the SNP did just this when it voted to oppose the loosening of Sunday trading laws in England. EVEL gave the ruling Conservatives an unfair advantage since it won a majority of English seats at the 2015, 2017 and 2019 general elections. Thus EVEL can allow a government to increase its dominance of Parliament.

Exam tip

Make sure you know which constitutional reforms occurred between 1997 and 2010, and which have occurred since 2010. Questions asking about constitutional reforms in the UK will specify a certain period. You therefore need to know which reforms can be included in your answer and which can be excluded.

The EU (Withdrawal Agreement) Act 2020 REVISED

+ This law confirmed the UK's withdrawal from the EU from 1 February 2020.
+ It allowed for a transition period whereby the UK would continue to participate in a number of EU programmes until the end of 2021.
+ It guaranteed the right of EU citizens living in the UK to stay in the country.
+ It included special provisions for Northern Ireland to avoid a 'hard border' with the Republic of Ireland.

It is too early to predict for certain the impact of this law and, more broadly, of the UK's decision to leave the EU. The EU is covered in more detail in Chapter 8. However, Table 5.15 gives some specific arguments on both sides of the debate in relation to the EU (Withdrawal Agreement) Act 2020.

Table 5.15 The positive and negative aspects of the EU (Withdrawal Agreement) Act 2020

Positive aspects	Negative aspects
The law respected the decision taken by the electorate in the EU referendum in 2016. It was given greater legitimacy by the Conservative Party's commanding victory in the 2019 general election, where the party had campaigned to 'get Brexit done'.	The passing of the Act may have been a victory for those who voted Leave, but it did little to bring the country together. Brexit remains a highly divisive issue and critics argue that the Act had few areas of compromise that would satisfy those who voted to remain.
The issue of Northern Ireland and the potential disruption to trade with the Republic of Ireland has been addressed, with Northern Ireland continuing to enforce EU rules on goods.	There now appears to be a completely different set of trading arrangements for one part of the UK compared with all the others. Not a single Northern Irish MP voted for the law.
The transition period allowed for the UK and the EU to prepare properly for the UK's departure from the EU single market, as well as from programmes relating to police cooperation and other matters.	The Act essentially put off most of the difficult decisions regarding the UK's future relationship with the EU, specifically the future trading relationship.

Remember

It is useful to have a clear idea of which constitutional reforms you think have worked well and which reforms you think have gone less well. Make a list of the reforms described on the previous pages, placing them in order from most successful to least successful.

Answers and quick quizzes at **www.hoddereducation.co.uk/myrevisionnotesdownloads**

13 Look at these post-1997 constitutional reforms. Was each one a Labour-led reform or a Conservative-led reform?

Reform	Government
Human Rights Act	Labour
Fixed-term Parliaments Act	
Constitutional Reform Act	
House of Lords Act	
Freedom of Information Act	
English Votes for English Laws Order	

Answers online

Debates on future constitutional reform

There have been several proposals to change the UK Constitution. Suggestions for parliamentary reform, such as electing the House of Lords, will be addressed in Chapter 6. Proposals for electoral reform have been examined in Chapter 3. This chapter will focus on three proposals for constitutional reform:

+ devolution for England
+ introducing a Bill of Rights to replace the Human Rights Act
+ a codified constitution

Devolution for England

 REVISED ◯

Despite the elections of city and regional mayors, and the establishment of new political structures such as the Greater London Authority, devolution in England has been far more limited than in Scotland, Wales and Northern Ireland. Two options for addressing this issue are to have an English Parliament or regional assemblies. Table 5.16 considers the arguments for and against establishing an English Parliament.

Table 5.16 Arguments for and against establishing an English Parliament

For	Against
England is the only nation in the UK not to have its own parliament, which has created resentment.	If every nation in the UK had its own parliament, it would raise the question of what the UK Parliament is for.
It could sit outside of London, reducing that city's political dominance and potentially reducing the North–South divide.	It would not give any more autonomy to the different regions in the UK. The people of Cornwall are likely to feel as distant from an English Parliament in, say, Nottingham as they are from the UK Parliament in Westminster.
An English Parliament would permanently resolve the West Lothian question. It would clarify what is meant by 'English-only' issues and leave the Westminster Parliament free to focus on truly national issues. The EVEL measure, introduced in 2015, did not go far enough, as non-English MPs can still vote on English-only matters.	The West Lothian question or English question has already been addressed by EVEL in 2015, which strikes the right balance between acknowledging that English MPs should have a greater say on matters relating to England and accepting that all laws passed in England have a considerable knock-on effect for the rest of the UK.
It can be argued that English identity and culture has been under threat from immigration and multiculturalism. An English Parliament would promote and preserve this.	Well under 20% of the public support the creation of an English Parliament, according to the latest opinion polls. Polls also suggest that most English voters say they wish to be governed from the Westminster Parliament.

The idea behind regional assemblies is that in each region in England there would be established an elected body with responsibility for a number of policy areas. These bodies would enjoy roughly similar power to each other. Table 5.17 considers the arguments for and against establishing regional assemblies.

Table 5.17 The arguments for and against regional assembles for England

For	Against
Supporters of regional assemblies claim they would better reflect regional identity than the UK government. They argue that central government frequently fails to understand regional sensitivities. They might point to an example such as the 'pasty tax', proposed by the government in 2012, which could have affected West Country businesses.	Only a few regions have a strong regional identity, such as Yorkshire and the West Country.
Regional authorities, rather than Westminster, are best placed to take decisions on tax and on other matters that involve regional needs.	Having regions in charge of taxes could lead to damaging tax competition in a bid to lure businesses to specific regions.
It would resolve the problem of asymmetric devolution. Currently, only some cities and metro regions have enjoyed devolved power in England. Regional assemblies would resolve this asymmetry by creating a more federal system. This would therefore correct the 'democratic deficit' that the current arrangements produce.	Asymmetric devolution is an appropriate model for a country such as the UK and a nation such as England. Some regions feel well served by the Westminster Parliament while others do not and so it is right that devolution is applied on a case-by-case basis. The new assemblies might result in a competition for power among existing devolved bodies.
There is cross-party support for regional devolution in England, as shown by a recent report supporting this model by the Political and Constitutional Reform Select Committee of the House of Commons.	There is only limited public support for regional assemblies. Voters in the northeast overwhelmingly rejected a North East Assembly in a 2004 referendum.

> **Now test yourself** TESTED
>
> 14 Explain one argument in favour of asymmetric devolution and one argument against.
>
> 15 Describe three arguments against further devolution in England.
>
> **Answers online**

Replacing the Human Rights Act with a British Bill of Rights

REVISED

Ever since the passing of the Human Rights Act in 1998, there has been criticism from both sides of the political spectrum.

Right-wing criticisms have focused on the rulings of the European Court of Human Rights (ECtHR) in Strasbourg, which interprets the European Convention on Human Rights (ECHR):
+ They claim that the Human Rights Act extends the scope of the ECHR still further, allowing domestic as well as foreign courts too much power over the decisions of elected politicians.
+ Therefore, a Bill of Rights could reduce the role that the ECHR and the courts play in domestic decision making.

Meanwhile, some on the left, notably liberal politicians, believe that the Act does not go far enough in defending the rights of the citizen against the state. They believe that anything that replaces the Human Rights Act should be entrenched.

Both conservative and liberal commentators have called for the Act to be replaced by a British Bill of Rights, although their visions of what that would contain are markedly different. Table 5.18 contains arguments in favour of and against replacing the Human Rights Act with a British Bill of Rights.

Table 5.18 Arguments in favour of and against replacing the Human Rights Act (HRA) with a British Bill of Rights

Arguments in favour	Arguments against
Critics of the HRA argue that judges in both Strasbourg and the UK are guilty of 'judicial overreach', weighing into areas that they say should be for elected politicians to decide.	Supporters of the HRA and ECHR argue that Conservatives overstate the influence of the ECtHR and that they do so because of a wider dislike of European influence and of citizens' rights more generally.
A Bill of Rights could clarify convention rights and how they should be applied in the UK. For example, the phrase 'degrading treatment and punishment' contained within the ECHR could be more narrowly defined.	An exercise in 'clarifying' rights could lead to rights being qualified and reduced where government and Parliament think fit.
Some rulings have been deeply unpopular, such as *Hirst* v *United Kingdom* (2005), where the ECtHR found that the UK had breached prisoners' rights by banning them from voting. Advocates of a Bill of Rights argue that it would restore faith and trust in a less interfering judiciary.	Human rights laws will inevitably frustrate governments in order to protect rights. To supporters of the HRA, that's no bad thing.
It is argued that the Strasbourg court and the HRA undermine the sovereignty of Parliament. For example, under Article 46 of the ECHR, the UK is required to implement the judgments of the ECtHR.	Parliament chooses which rulings to follow. Despite its ruling on allowing prisoner rights, Parliament is yet to change the law.
Some argue that a Bill of Rights would reflect the balance between rights and responsibilities in a twenty-first-century world. For example, it could recognise the right to privacy but allow governments flexibility to counter terrorism, much of which is orchestrated through encrypted messages on social media platforms.	Those against scrapping the HRA argue that any repeal of the Act will signal a British retreat from the postwar human rights architecture, which they claim has done much to encourage the nations of Europe and beyond to adhere to basic human rights standards.
Left-wing supporters of a Bill of Rights argue that it does not have to reflect a Conservative tradition but instead a more liberal and tolerant one.	There is no unity on what would go into a British Bill of Rights. The fact that the HRA has been attacked by the left and the right could show that it gets the balance right between protecting rights and preserving parliamentary sovereignty.
The current HRA lacks entrenchment. This is why it can be altered and likely weakened by the 2019 Tory manifesto pledge to 'update' the HRA.	

> **Remember**
>
> It is important to understand the link between the Human Rights Act, the European Convention on Human Rights (ECHR) and the European Court of Human Rights in Strasbourg. The Strasbourg court interprets the ECHR. The Human Rights Act gave courts in the UK the power to do the same.

The codification debate

REVISED ○

The arguments as to whether the UK Constitution should be codified mainly focus on the trade-off between flexibility and greater protection of rights. Additional arguments are outlined in Table 5.19.

Table 5.19 Arguments against and in favour of codifying the UK Constitution

Arguments against	Arguments in favour
It may undermine existing political structures that have worked well. Parliamentary sovereignty would almost certainly be undermined.	Rights would be better protected. Example: Labour extended the detention-without-trial period while the Conservatives passed the Investigatory Powers Act that increases the ability of the state to obtain data from UK citizens. A codified constitution would establish the rights of citizens, and the laws mentioned above could be struck down if they encroached upon these rights.
The UK could lose flexibility in its constitutional arrangements. States in the USA have had sensible restrictions on carrying handguns struck down because of the second amendment right to bear arms, while the UK was able to very quickly introduce restrictions on the sale of guns after the 1996 Dunblane massacre.	A codified constitution doesn't have to be inflexible: France has a codified constitution but has changed it on many occasions.
The uncodified constitution allows the government to govern. The 2019 general election gave the UK government a clear mandate to 'get Brexit done' and thus restore political certainty, a quality that can only come with strong government that can take decisive action.	An entrenched constitution would act as a brake on executive power, preventing single-party initiatives such as the abolition of the Greater London Council and six metropolitan counties by Margaret Thatcher.
A codified constitution like that of the USA might thrust the Supreme Court into political issues and so threaten its neutrality and independence.	It would bolster the ability of the courts to hold the government to account.
There is uncertainty as to who would write it and what would go in it. In all likelihood, existing arrangements would simply be written down in one place, so that executive power would be codified but not reduced. Doing such a thing would thus increase governmental power — the very thing that codified constitutions are supposed to limit.	A codified constitution would lead to greater clarity. Constitutions are not difficult to create. They typically contain (a) rights, (b) the limits on government, (c) the powers of political institutions and (d) amendment procedures.

Revision activity

Make sure you thoroughly revise:
+ three arguments in favour of introducing a codified UK Constitution
+ three arguments against introducing a codified UK Constitution
+ two possible ways in which a codified constitution could be entrenched in the UK

Exam practice

1 Evaluate the view that the devolution process has successfully enhanced democracy in the UK. [30]
2 Evaluate the view that the UK is now effectively a federal system. [30]
3 Using the source, evaluate the view that the case for introducing a codified constitution has become overwhelming. [30]

There are a number of reasons why the introduction of a codified constitution remains an objective of liberal-minded politicians and constitutional experts.

Devolution has been created unevenly. It may, therefore, be time to codify the ways in which such powers are distributed. In addition, the whole status of referendums (increasingly used) needs to be clarified. Are they binding or are they not? On a broader level, we can ask the question of whether it is realistic today to view the UK Parliament as sovereign. If it is not, in reality, sovereign, then we need to clarify where sovereignty lies. The return of sovereignty after Brexit, too, presents a need to clarify this issue. There are also the older arguments that the constitution should be codified to protect citizens' rights more effectively and to prevent the creeping increase in unchecked executive power.

→

Answers and quick quizzes at **www.hoddereducation.co.uk/myrevisionnotesdownloads**

Nevertheless, critics argue that these arguments are outweighed by other considerations. We would, for example, be exchanging the known for the unknown, something that conservatives are instinctively concerned about. Above all, however, it is the flexibility of the UK's ancient uncodified constitution that exercises the minds of such critics most vigorously. 'We do not want,' they argue, 'to find ourselves in a position like that of the USA, where the entrenched and codified constitution acts as a block on many important reforms such as changes to the gun laws and socialised healthcare.' Our flexible constitution, they add, is a strength, not a weakness.

Source: original material

In your response you must:
+ compare and contrast the different opinions in the source
+ examine and debate these views in a balanced way
+ analyse and evaluate only the information presented in the source

Answers and quick quiz 5 online

Exam skills

+ For the Paper 2 essay (non-source only), you are required to use synoptic links. What this means is that you need to refer to content — specifically key terms — from Paper 1.
+ This requirement should not be seen as too onerous — you only have to mention *one* Paper 1 word on *one* occasion in your essay and there is no requirement to do so for the source-based question.
+ If you forget to mention a synoptic link, your essay can only receive a maximum of 24 marks — it would be capped at the top of level 4.
+ Therefore, to give yourself every opportunity to receive a level-5 mark (25–30 marks) in the non-source-based essay, it is important to provide one synoptic link.
+ To provide one, it is good practice when you are planning your essay to make a list of a few Paper 1 terms that might be relevant for the essay question you are being asked.

The table below provides a suggested list of synoptic links that can be used for Question 1 from the Exam practice box above: 'Evaluate the view that the devolution process has successfully enhanced democracy in the UK.'

Synoptic link from Paper 1	How it could be applied
Legitimacy	The newly devolved bodies have been given added **legitimacy** because they were established with the consent of the people through referendums.
Referendums	Welsh voters have demonstrated their gradual acceptance of the new political structures by voting in a **referendum** to give the Welsh Assembly more power.
Participation crisis	Turnout for the devolved bodies remains low, adding to claims that they have not addressed the **participation crisis**.
Franchise	The devolved bodies have extended the **franchise**. With the exception of general elections, Scottish and Welsh 16- and 17-year-olds now have the right to vote.

Summary

You should now have an understanding of:
+ the nature and principles of the UK Constitution, specifically the lack of entrenchment and codification, its unitary nature, the rule of law, the fusion of powers and parliamentary sovereignty
+ how the nature and principles of the Constitution have been affected by recent constitutional reforms
+ the details of constitutional reforms since 1997 and the positive and negative aspects of each
+ the nature and context of devolution, and how it differs across the UK
+ the impact of devolution, both positive and negative
+ debates about future constitutional reform issues, including English devolution and the future of the Human Rights Act
+ the debate about whether the UK should have a codified constitution

The structure of the House of Commons

The House of Commons is known as the 'lower house' and is the elected half of Parliament. The structure of the House of Commons is as follows:

+ **650 Members of Parliament.**
+ **Frontbench MPs** — government ministers, senior and junior, plus leading spokespersons from opposition parties (about 150).
+ **Backbench MPs** — all those MPs who are not frontbenchers (about 500).
+ Select committees — permanent committees of backbench MPs, elected by all the MPs. Their main role is to scrutinise the work of government departments.
+ **Legislative committees** (also called public bill committees) — temporary committees that scrutinise proposed legislation and propose amendments to improve the legislation. They mostly have 20–40 members who are chosen by party whips.
+ **Party whips** — senior MPs who seek to persuade backbenchers in their own party to vote the way the party leadership wants them to, ensuring party unity.
+ **The Speaker** — presides over disputes in the House of Commons and takes decisions on parliamentary procedure.

House of Commons The elected and most powerful chamber of Parliament. Its membership consists of 650 MPs.

Parliament A name given to the legislature in many countries. It has the dual role of legitimising proposed legislation and representing the people.

Select committee A permanent committee of backbench MPs that scrutinises the work of government departments.

Public bill committees Also referred to as legislative committees, these are temporary committees established to give line-by-line scrutiny of a specific bill and to propose amendments.

The structure of the House of Lords

The House of Lords is known as the 'upper house' and is the unelected half of Parliament. It contains about 800 peers, of the following types:

+ **Hereditary peers** have inherited the title from their father and in most cases the title passes on to their sons (just a handful of hereditary peerages are passed through the female line). Out of the several thousand hereditary peers who live in the UK, only 92 are allowed to sit in the House of Lords.
+ **Life peers** are appointed for life by party leaders and an Appointments Commission. They do not pass on their title to their children. These peers are a mixture of former politicians and experts in various fields. Most peers have allegiance to a political party.
+ While most peers (both life and hereditary) have a party allegiance, some have no party affiliation and are fully independent. These peers are called **crossbench MPs.**
+ In addition to life and hereditary peers, **archbishops and bishops of the Church of England** are also members of the House of Lords. There are 26 of these. No other religions have automatic representation.
+ **The Lord Speaker** presides over debates in the House and maintains discipline.

House of Lords The unelected chamber of Parliament. Its main role is to examine and revise legislation from the House of Commons.

Remember

When one hereditary peer dies or retires from the House of Lords, there is a by-election among the chamber's remaining hereditary peers from the deceased's political party, who choose from the wider pool of hereditary peers (those who used to sit in the Lords until they were removed) to fill the vacancy. Critics point to the hypocrisy of maintaining the most undemocratic element of the Lords — the hereditary principle — with an election.

Making links

When referring to hereditary peers in the House of Lords, refer to the 'democratic deficit'.

The legislative process: House of Commons

The key stages in processing a legislative bill into law are outlined in Table 6.1.

Table 6.1 How a bill becomes law

Stage	Detail
First reading	MPs are informed about the bill or proposed legislation.
Second reading	The main debate on the bill is held, which is followed by a vote.
Committee stage	If the Commons votes in favour of the bill at the second reading, a public bill committee is formed to consider it line by line. This committee may propose amendments.
Report stage	The bill is debated again, with all the passed amendments included.
Third reading	There is a final debate and a last opportunity to block the legislation.
Passage to 'the other place' (House of Lords)	Most bills are first presented in the House of Commons, so they next pass to the House of Lords (though it can be the other way round). The procedures for passing the bill are roughly the same in the House of Lords.
Royal assent	The monarch signs the bill into the law, which signifies the formal passage of the bill into the law. It is now an Act of Parliament.

> **Legislative bill** A proposal presented to Parliament for legislation. Once passed in Parliament, a bill becomes an Act of Parliament.

The nature of parliamentary bills

Table 6.2 shows the types of legislation which pass through Parliament, with their descriptions.

Table 6.2 Types of legislation

Type of legislation	Description
Public bills	These are bills presented by the government. They are expected to pass successfully into law.
Primary legislation	These are major pieces of legislation either changing the law or granting powers to subsidiary bodies and individuals to make secondary legislation.
Secondary legislation (also called delegated legislation)	These are usually described as ministerial orders. Under powers granted in primary legislation, ministers or other bodies may make minor regulations on their own. Most such orders are not debated in Parliament, but Parliament has the option of vetoing such legislation.
Private members' bills	Backbench MPs may enter a ballot allowing five of them each year to present their own proposed piece of legislation. These rarely pass into law unless they receive the support of government. There is usually not enough parliamentary time to consider them.
Private bills	Such bills are presented by individuals or organisations outside government and Parliament. They apply to Parliament for permission to take certain actions (often building or changing land use) which are currently forbidden.

MPs

You should know the following key points about MPs:
+ MPs all represent a constituency.
+ Virtually all MPs are part of a specific political party, although some MPs have been elected as 'independent' MPs in the past.
+ MPs enjoy parliamentary privilege, which means they are free from outside interference and cannot be prosecuted or sued for anything they say within the House of Commons.
+ MPs who are not members of the government or the leadership of their party are known as backbenchers.

> **Parliamentary privilege** An ancient principle that protects MPs from external pressure and specifically means they cannot be prosecuted or sued for anything they may say in the House of Commons. It also implies that the monarch can never interfere with the work of the UK Parliament.
>
> **Backbenchers** MPs and peers who are not senior members of their party and so sit in Parliament behind the front bench.

The functions of backbench MPs   REVISED ◯

Backbench MPs have the following functions:
+ They can initiate legislation through private members' bills. These are not bills that have the backing of the government but are instead introduced by individual backbench MPs.
+ They represent the interests of their constituents.
+ They can threaten a backbench rebellion by voting against the wishes of their party leadership.
+ They can scrutinise government policy and decisions.
+ They can take positions of leadership in the House of Commons by becoming select committee chairs.
+ They can ask parliamentary questions and take part in debates.

> **Private members' bills**
> Legislation introduced by individual backbench MPs. These bills do not necessarily have the backing of government.

How influential are backbench MPs?   REVISED ◯

Table 6.3 considers the influence and limitations of backbench MPs.

Table 6.3 The influence of backbench MPs

Influence	Limitations on influence
Backbenchers have been increasingly willing to 'defy the whip' and vote against the government, helping the Commons to hold the government to account. Example: in 2020 thirty-eight Tory backbenchers voted against government plans to allow Huawei to be used in the UK's 5G mobile network. While the government won the vote, it changed its policy shortly afterwards.	Party whips still control the vast majority of voting outcomes and backbench MPs are loath to risk a future promotion by voting against their party leadership. It is very rare for a backbench rebellion to lead to a defeat of a majority government.
The creation of the Backbench Business Committee (BBC) has allowed backbenchers a greater say on which issues are raised and discussed in the House of Commons. Example: in December 2020 the BBC secured a debate on raising awareness about teenage cancer.	Many of the debates that the BBC wins time for are held in Westminster Hall and not in the House of Commons. The debates held in Westminster do not enjoy the same status as those held in the House of Commons. There is often no vote after these debates and so their influence is limited.

Influence	Limitations on influence
Backbenchers have more influence in hung parliaments, increasing their ability to call into question the actions of government. Example: between 2017 and 2019, when no party enjoyed a majority, the Speaker accepted a far higher number of urgent questions, which allow backbench MPs to summon ministers to the House of Commons to answer questions on an urgent matter.	Backbenchers have less influence when the government has a majority, as rebellions can be more easily overcome.

Now test yourself   TESTED ⬤

5   Give three ways that backbenchers can influence decision making.

6   Give three limits to backbench influence.

Answers online

Revision activity

Revise good examples of the work of MPs. Include work:

1   in relation to their constituencies

2   in committees

Exam tip

If the question you answer refers to 'Parliament', it is important to include information about both chambers — the House of Commons and the House of Lords.

Peers

Peers perform the following functions:

+ They represent different sections of society in Parliament, including ethnic minorities, the elderly, hospital patients and the various professions.

+ They advocate in favour of important political causes, ensuring that they are given as much publicity as possible. Typical causes include environmental issues, human rights concerns and animal welfare.

+ Peers with special expertise play a valuable role in examining proposed legislation.

+ Every government department has a frontbench representative in the Lords, which gives peers the opportunity to call government to account, although this function receives less publicity than its equivalent activity in the Commons.

Exam tip

When you write about how the House of Lords stands up for vulnerable sections of society, use specific examples of peers doing this and outline exactly what they have done. Here are two examples:

+ Lord Dubs helped to amend the 2016 Immigration Act to allow child refugees arriving from Calais the right to remain in the UK.

+ Baroness Oona King played a leading role in attempts to increase funding for post-adoption services and exempt parents who have adopted children from cuts to benefits.

Now test yourself   TESTED ⬤

7   Describe two functions of a backbench MP in the House of Commons.

8   Describe two functions of a peer in the House of Lords.

Answers online

Functions of the House of Commons

The House of Commons has three main functions:

+ **Scrutiny.** This involves examining the work of government and holding it to account for its actions. Scrutiny can entail criticising government actions, forcing ministers to explain policy and perhaps even dismissing a government through a vote of no confidence.

+ **Passing and examining legislation, often referred to as the legislative function.** Any proposed legislation is examined by MPs. They may make amendments to improve the legislation and to protect the interests of minorities. This function overlaps with the scrutiny function, since Parliament should ensure that only worthwhile laws are passed, without preventing government from functioning. It is a delicate balance to perform.

Vote of no confidence

A motion that, if passed, will effectively dismiss the government and force an election. If a vote of no confidence is defeated, it implies that Parliament has confidence in the government of the day. Theresa May's administration survived a vote of no confidence in January 2019.

93

+ **Representation.** MPs are expected to ensure that the interests of their constituencies are protected — both the interests of the constituency as a whole and those of individual constituents. We can also consider representation in terms of resemblance.

In addition to these three main functions, the House of Commons provides the role of legitimation (in a sense, the Commons is granting consent on behalf of the people when it votes in favour of bills). The Commons also provides a deliberative function (it is the forum for national debate).

> **Resemblance** The idea that representative institutions should be staffed by people who come from a wide variety of backgrounds and professions and who share similar characteristics with the communities they serve. For example, there should be equal numbers of women and men.

Functions of the House of Lords

The House of Lords has similar functions to the House of Commons but these functions are more limited or conducted in a different manner:

+ **Scrutiny.** The Lords cannot veto a piece of legislation but it can force the government to re-present it the following year. This power of delay effectively forces government to think again for a year and possibly add amendments to make the legislation acceptable.
+ **Legislative function.** The Lords plays a crucial role in revising bills that are sent from the House of Commons. The fact that the chamber contains so many experts makes this process especially meaningful.
+ **Representation.** While the House of Lords is unelected, it has gained a reputation for standing up for the rights of minorities and vulnerable groups.

Powers of the House of Commons

The House of Commons has the exclusive power to:

+ approve or reject proposed legislation
+ dismiss a government through a vote of no confidence
+ order ministers to answer questions on the floor of the house, in a select committee or in writing
+ amend legislation
+ order debates on important national issues or in a crisis or emergency

Backbench MPs may introduce private members' bills for consideration.

Powers of the House of Lords

The House of Lords has the power to:

+ delay the passage of legislation for up to a year
+ amend legislation, although such amendments may be overturned in the House of Commons
+ order a government minister (if the minister is a member of the House of Lords rather than the House of Commons) to answer questions on government policies and decisions
+ debate issues of great national concern

Now test yourself   TESTED ⭘

9 Explain three exclusive powers of the House of Commons.

10 Explain three powers of the House of Lords.

Answers online

Distinctions between the House of Commons and the House of Lords

Since the House of Lords is unelected, three main limits have been placed on its power:

+ The Parliament Act 1911 banned the Lords from having legislative control over financial matters. This ban confirmed the elected Commons' 'financial privilege'.
+ The Parliament Act 1949 stipulated that the Lords can only delay the passage of legislation for one year.
+ The Salisbury Convention, dating back to the 1940s, means that the Lords cannot obstruct any proposed legislation that was contained in the governing party's last election manifesto.

Table 6.4 outlines the powers of the two chambers.

Salisbury Convention A convention that ensures major government bills that are mentioned in an election manifesto will not be voted down by the House of Lords. It acknowledges that the unelected House of Lords lacks the legitimacy to block bills that a winning party pledged to introduce at the last general election.

Table 6.4 The key differences in powers of the House of Commons and House of Lords

The power to...	House of Commons	House of Lords
veto proposed legislation	Yes	No — only the power to delay for one year, as set out in the Parliament Act 1949
amend legislation	Yes	Yes, but these amendments can be rejected by the House of Commons
call ministers to account in select committees	Yes	No
dismiss a government through a vote of no confidence	Yes	No
propose and amend budgets	Yes	No — due to rules on financial privilege
introduce and scrutinise legislation in a government's manifesto	Yes	No — due to the Salisbury Convention

Exam tip

You may be asked to compare the House of Commons and House of Lords. It is important to use comparative language to ensure that both chambers are mentioned and compared in every paragraph. Words such as 'similarly' or 'whereas' are useful as they remind you to do this. Here are three examples of sentences that use comparative language:

+ The House of Commons has the power to veto legislation *whereas* the House of Lords can only delay legislation for up to one year.
+ The House of Commons can amend legislation, *similar* to the Lords.
+ However, *unlike* the Lords, the House of Commons can strike down amendments from the other chamber.

The role and significance of the opposition

Parliament interacts with the government in a number of ways (through the actions of backbenchers, tabling of questions etc.), including through the official opposition and the work it does to hold the government to account.

The general term opposition refers to the following features:

+ All MPs and peers who are not members of the governing party may be described as 'opposition MPs and peers'.
+ The 'official opposition' is the second largest party in the House of Commons.

Opposition A general term referring to all parties that are not part of the government. 'Her Majesty's official opposition' refers to the second largest party in the House of Commons.

+ The leader of that party is described as 'leader of the opposition'.
+ The leader of the opposition has special privileges, notably to speak in debates and to take the main role at Prime Minister's Questions.

The role of the opposition includes:
+ forcing the government to explain and justify its policies and decisions
+ highlighting the shortcomings of the way the government is running the country
+ presenting alternative proposals to those of the government if appropriate
+ making itself ready to be an alternative government if the current government is defeated at the next general election
+ setting the parliamentary agenda on supply days, of which there are normally around 20 per year, whereby the opposition may debate any issue it wants and even hold votes

> **Supply days** Also known as opposition days, these are parliamentary days that are under the control of opposition parties rather than the government.

Ministerial questions and accountability

All government ministers interact with Parliament by appearing before the Commons on a regular basis to answer questions. Ministers who are peers also have to appear regularly in the Lords. Table 6.5 describes the most frequent types of questions that are asked.

Table 6.5 Parliamentary questions

Type of question	Description
Ministerial questions	Secretaries of state and ministers from government departments are required to answer questions from opposition MPs in the shadow cabinet and from backbenchers on issues relating to their department.
Prime Minister's Questions (PMQs)	PMQs is held every week, during which the prime minister is questioned by the leader of the opposition and backbench MPs.
Urgent questions (UQs)	These are questions that are asked by an MP (usually from the opposing party) and deemed by the Speaker to be of pressing public interest, and which need to be discussed immediately.
Written questions	MPs and peers can ask government ministers written questions. These are often used to gather a more detailed response or clarify statistical information.

> **Prime Minister's Questions (PMQs)** Session that gives backbench MPs and leaders of opposition parties the chance to ask the prime minister questions. It takes place every Wednesday.

Now test yourself   TESTED ◯

11 Look at the following types of parliamentary questions and describe what they involve.

Parliamentary questions	Description
Written questions	
Prime Minister's Questions (PMQs)	
Urgent questions (UQs)	

Answers online

The effectiveness of Parliament

To assess the effectiveness of Parliament, it is important to consider how well it performs its three main functions, which are:

+ its legislative function
+ its representative function
+ its scrutiny function

Tables 6.6–6.8 provide an assessment of these functions.

Table 6.6 An assessment of how well Parliament performs its legislative function

It is effective	It is ineffective
Parliament has a high level of **legislative output**: the fusion of powers allows the government to dominate Parliament, thus allowing laws to be passed.	Parliament does not produce bills of a sufficient **legislative quality**: governments with large majorities often rush through legislation without appropriate scrutiny.
The House of Commons provides plenty of ways for backbench MPs to influence decision making, thereby improving the quality of legislation. For example, private members' bills give opportunities to backbenchers to make law. The Abortion Act and the Murder (Abolition of Death Penalty) Act were first introduced as private members' bills.	The government often dominates the legislative agenda, which is demonstrated by the minimal time given to private members' bills. Only around 6% of these bills ever become law.
The House of Lords ensures that legislation is suitably revised and thereby ensures legislative quality. In 2020 the House of Lords tabled amendments to the Agriculture Bill to increase safeguards on food imports.	The House of Lords is limited in its ability to revise laws. The House of Commons can simply defeat amendments proposed by the Lords, which is what happened to amendments attached to the EU Withdrawal Bill 2020.

Legislative output The number of bills that are enacted into law.

Legislative quality Refers to a situation whereby bills have received appropriate scrutiny and have not been rushed through Parliament.

Remember

It is incredibly difficult to even bring a private members' bill to the floor of the Commons. MPs get a chance to draft a bill through a random draw of lots. Parliamentary rules mean it only requires one MP to shout 'object' to a private members' bill to block its progress. In 2018 Conservative MP Christopher Chope shouted 'object' on a bill to ban upskirting and in 2019 on a proposed bill to outlaw female genital mutilation.

Table 6.7 An assessment of how well Parliament performs its representative function

It is effective	It is ineffective
Arguably, Parliament does indeed resemble the people it serves. The number of female MPs has risen from 118 in 2001 to 220 in 2019. The number of black, Asian and minority ethnic (BAME) MPs has increased from 41 in 2015 to 63 after the 2019 general election.	There is still a great deal of work to be done for both chambers to truly reflect the demographics of the nation. Only 34% of MPs and barely a quarter of peers are women. Less than 10% of MPs are from a minority ethnic background.
Elections to the House of Commons help Parliament to reflect sudden shifts in public opinion. The Conservatives enjoyed a net gain of 47 seats at the 2019 general election, which perhaps reflected a desire among the public to end the gridlock over Brexit.	The first-past-the-post electoral system produces unfair results. The 2015 general election delivered the most disproportional result since the 1920s. UKIP won 3.8 million votes but only one seat. The House of Lords remains unelected.
Multiple parties enjoy representation in Westminster. There are ten parties whose MPs take their seats in Parliament. There are also crossbenchers in the Lords.	The electoral system and the role of the whips hinder multi-party politics. The two main parties control 87% of the seats in the House of Commons. The 2019 general election saw no independent MPs elected to the House of Commons.
Parliamentarians stand up for the people they serve. MPs hold regular surgeries for their constituents. They have been particularly active in helping constituents access help to immigration advice, especially since the vote to leave the EU has created uncertainty for non-UK nationals from the EU.	Parliamentarians are far more likely to consider their own careers above those who elected them. MPs owe their selection as a candidate to their party, not their constituents. The majority of MPs vote in accordance with the wishes of the party leadership.

Table 6.8 An assessment of how well Parliament performs its scrutiny function

It is effective	It is ineffective
Parliamentary questions can help ensure accountability. Urgent questions (UQs) are a particularly useful way of scrutinising government ministers, since they require ministers to attend and answer at short notice. Between the 2017 general election and February 2019, the then Speaker John Bercow allowed 173 UQs to be tabled.	Some forms of parliamentary questions are less useful in holding the government to account. PMQs has been described as a 'Punch and Judy show' by David Cameron. Governments often ask their own backbenchers to ask 'planted' questions, which are easy for the prime minister to answer.
A united opposition can provide effective scrutiny of the government and force changes in government policy. In 2009 the opposition defeated the government on the issue of whether Nepalese Gurkha soldiers should have the right of residence in the UK. It utilised its supply days in order to do so.	The opposition is often quite divided between the various parties that make it up. The official opposition party may also be further divided internally. Labour splits on whether to launch military action against ISIS in 2015 allowed the government to win an easy majority, when 66 Labour MPs voted in favour of airstrikes.
The House of Lords has become more effective at scrutinising the government, due to the absence of a Conservative majority. The crossbenchers hold the balance of power in the chamber. Between 2017 and 2019, the government suffered 69 defeats in the House of Lords.	There are limits to the House of Lords' scrutiny role, including the Parliament Acts, rules of financial privilege and the Salisbury Convention. The fact that '**parliamentary ping-pong**' was curtailed over the EU Withdrawal Act 2020 owed much to the unelected Lords' own awareness that they were challenging a government with a large Commons majority and a fresh mandate to 'get Brexit done'.
A minority government, relying on **confidence and supply** deals, is likely to face increased scrutiny, as it will find it difficult to win over enough MPs from opposing parties to win a majority in any given vote. The passing of the Benn Act in 2019 required the government to seek an extension to Brexit if no deal on the UK's future relationship with the EU could be reached by the initial deadline to leave on 31 October.	A government with a large majority tends to limit the effectiveness of parliamentary scrutiny. It is harder for the opposition to muster the required votes to defeat the government on any given piece of legislation. Between 1997 and 2004 the Labour government, with its huge parliamentary majority, did not face a single defeat in the House of Commons.

Confidence and supply An arrangement between the governing party and a smaller party in a hung parliament whereby the smaller party agrees to support the government in key votes, such as on the budget and on votes of no confidence. In return, the smaller party usually secures support on a specific policy.

Parliamentary ping-pong Occurs when the two houses cannot agree on the wording of a bill, which is then sent back and forth between the two chambers for amendments.

Now test yourself

TESTED ○

12 Provide a counter-argument to each of the arguments given below.

Argument	Counter-argument
Parliament has a high level of legislative output.	
Parliament is now more socially representative — for instance, there are more women in Parliament than ever before.	
Hung parliaments have resulted in increased scrutiny of government decisions.	

Answers online

Remember

The term 'whip' is used in a variety of ways. 'Party whips' are MPs appointed by the party leadership to persuade MPs of the same party to vote in line with party policy. A 'three-line whip' is a strict instruction to vote in accordance with the leadership's wishes and failure to do so may see the 'whip being removed' from an MP, which means that they are effectively expelled from the party and sit as an independent until the whip is restored.

Parliamentary committees

There are several different kinds of parliamentary committee, each of which assists Parliament to perform its function of scrutinising government. The two most important types of committee that sit in the House of Commons are select committees and public bill committees.

Select committees

REVISED

+ Select committees scrutinise the work of each department in terms of efficiency, effectiveness, fairness and value for money.
+ There are 11–15 members on each committee who are chosen by the whole House.
+ The chair, who can be from any political party and who enjoys an increased salary, is elected by a secret ballot.
+ The governing party has a majority on each committee.
+ Select committees publish reports that usually contain a number of recommendations for the government to consider. The government must respond to these reports within 2 months.

Table 6.9 considers the effectiveness of select committees in holding the government to account.

Table 6.9 The effectiveness of select committees

They are effective	They are ineffective
Select committee reports are taken seriously by government. The government accepts an estimated 40% of select committee recommendations.	They can only *advise* the government by making recommendations, which are non-binding and usually only concern minor changes in policy.
They have the power to gather written and oral evidence and to summon witnesses, including ministers, civil servants, experts and members of the public with a relevant interest.	Select committees' powers to compel witnesses to appear and to tell the truth seem weak and undefined. In 2013 as home secretary, Theresa May blocked the Home Affairs Select Committee from interviewing the head of MI5, Andrew Parker.
Select committees enjoy a good deal of freedom from government interference. Government ministers, opposition frontbenchers and party whips do not serve in select committees, meaning that such committees give voice to backbench concerns.	The governing party has a majority of seats on every committee and chairs may not always be independent from the departments they are supposed to scrutinise. Former health secretary Jeremy Hunt's election as chair of the Health Select Committee in 2020 raised doubts about how well he would want to hold his former department to account given that he introduced most of that department's policies in the previous years.
The work carried out by committees is consensual rather than combative in nature; MPs are generally not concerned with political point-scoring.	Not all committees work by consensus. The Exiting the EU Committee lacked cross-party cohesion. In May 2018 Conservative committee members publicly criticised it for being too pro-Remain. These divides allowed the government to ignore many of the recommendations made by the committee.
Chairing a select committee has become a viable alternative career to that of becoming a minister. Yvette Cooper, chair of the Home Affairs Select Committee, seemingly gave up a career on the Labour front bench and opted instead for a role that involves intricate scrutiny of government policy.	The prospect of promotion to the government could potentially still get in the way of effective scrutiny. The former chair of the Home Affairs Select Committee, Rory Stewart, became a prisons minister in Theresa May's government. This example shows that the lure of a government payroll job can still outweigh the status of a committee assignment.

> **Remember**
>
> The Public Accounts Committee (PAC) is perhaps the most important select committee. It scrutinises value for money of public spending and generally holds the government and its civil servants to account for the delivery of public services. Its reports are often unanimous in their conclusions, so it stands above party politics.

Public bill committees

+ These committees are temporary and are established to examine a bill, providing line-by-line scrutiny.
+ Their membership is heavily influenced by the whips.
+ These committees are established after the second reading, and therefore after there has been a vote to proceed with the bill's passage through Parliament.

Table 6.10 considers the effectiveness of public bill committees in holding the government to account.

Table 6.10 The effectiveness of public bill committees

They are effective	They are not effective
They provide detailed, line-by-line examination of a bill and can propose amendments. This task allows the committees to consider problems with the legislation that were not picked up in the earlier readings.	Government whips can completely dominate proceedings, with the committee majority accepting only government amendments. Around 99% of ministerial amendments succeed, while the success rate for non-government amendments is below 1%. Bill committees are involved at the latter stages of the legislative process, once there has already been a Commons vote at the second reading. The legislation is therefore already considered a 'done deal'.
The ministers attending come from the department involved and are matched by the shadow cabinet frontbenchers who parallel them, and this brings a certain degree of different expertise to each discussion.	Bill committees may lack expertise because their membership is heavily controlled by party whips. In 2011 Sarah Wollaston, a Conservative backbench MP who had worked for 24 years as a doctor, was prevented from sitting on the public bill committee scrutinising changes to the NHS. It was claimed that she would be too critical of government policy.

Other Commons committees

Other notable committees in the House of Commons are the following:
+ The Liaison Committee is made up of all the chairs of the departmental select committees. Twice a year this committee questions the prime minister extensively and sometimes quite aggressively over key aspects of government policy.
+ The Backbench Business Committee determines the business of the House for more than 20 days a year. It decides what backbenchers will debate on those days.
+ The Petitions Committee looks at e-petitions and considers how to respond to them. It can put forward a petition for debate in the House of Commons or press the government for action.

Remember

Be careful not to confuse select committees with public bill committees. Legislative committees exclusively consider amendments to proposed legislation, while select committees call government to account. Critics of committees argue that to have more influence, the roles of both committees should be merged.

Now test yourself TESTED ○

13 Complete the table by listing which parliamentary committee performs the function stated.

Function	Committee
Questions the prime minister extensively on two occasions per year	
Considers which e-petitions ought to be considered for debate in the House of Commons	
Provides detailed, line-by-line examination of a bill and can propose amendments	
Shadows the work of government departments	

Answers online

6 Parliament

The reform of Parliament

There are a number of debates concerning the reform of Parliament. The key potential reform for the House of Commons would be a change in the electoral system to one that is more proportional. This reform is addressed in Chapter 3. However, given the decisive rejection of electoral reform in a 2011 referendum, it is unlikely to be embraced in the near future.

In the House of Lords, the main debate has centred around whether members should be elected. The background to this debate is as follows:

✦ The Labour government completed the first stage of House of Lords reform in 1999 by removing most hereditary peers.

✦ The second stage of this reform was to introduce an elected element.

✦ This second stage failed to be completed because politicians could not choose between having a fully elected chamber to maximise democratic legitimacy or a partly elected chamber to keep in the House of Lords people who have amassed special expertise.

Table 6.11 summarises arguments in favour of and against an elected House of Lords.

Table 6.11 Arguments in favour of and against electing members of the House of Lords

Arguments against electing members of the House of Lords	Arguments in favour of electing members of the House of Lords
The hereditary peers, the most undemocratic element of the House of Lords, have largely been removed by the first stage of reforms.	There are still 92 hereditary peers who remain and vote on a regular basis. Lesotho is the only other country in the world that maintains the hereditary principle in its legislature.
The current balance and composition of the House of Lords, with no single party enjoying a majority, allows it to provide a useful check on the government. Electing the chamber could produce a government majority in both houses.	The Lords would be able to stand up to the government more if it enjoyed greater democratic legitimacy, rather than being sidelined due to the Salisbury Convention.
Elections would likely remove the wisdom, experience and independence of thought of peers. The current chamber benefits from the presence of ex-ministers and other experts, willing to stand up for unpopular but worthwhile causes.	The lack of social diversity and the regional imbalance of the Lords (most peers live in London and the southeast) could be addressed with an elected chamber. The needs of minority groups and of the various UK regions would therefore be better met.
An elected House of Lords could result in gridlock, since the Parliament Acts that limit the chamber's powers would become unjustified. Systems with coequal legislative chambers, such as the US system, often find it difficult to pass budgets.	Having two elected chambers that challenge each other could prevent executive dominance

Now test yourself

TESTED

14 Identify two arguments in favour of electing members of the House of Lords.

15 Identify two arguments in favour of retaining the unelected House of Lords.

Answers online

Exam practice

1 Evaluate the view that the House of Lords performs a meaningful role in UK democracy. [30]

2 Evaluate the view that Parliament is able effectively to call government to account. [30]

3 Using the source, evaluate the view that the House of Lords is more representative than the House of Commons. [30]

It is often suggested that the reason the House of Commons has more status than the House of Lords is because it is genuinely representative while the House of Lords is certainly not. This is really for just one overwhelming reason: the Commons is elected but the Lords is not. If we look more deeply, however, the assertion can be challenged.

→

My Revision Notes: Pearson Edexcel A-Level Politics: UK politics second edition

The electoral system used for general elections ensures that the representation of parties in the Commons is disproportionate. The parties with concentrated support — Labour, Conservative and Scottish Nationalist — have a disproportionally large representation, while those with dispersed support, such as the Liberal Democrats, are heavily under-represented. It is also true that the House of Commons contains too few women (about a quarter) and too few members of ethnic minorities in relation to the whole population.

The unelected, unaccountable House of Lords seems, at first sight, to be remarkably undemocratic. However, it is undeniably true that the representation of parties in the Lords is more accurate than it is in the Commons, with a large group of Liberal Democrats present and some representation for small parties. The social make-up of the Lords is similar to that of the Commons, too. But it is in the representation of minority interests that the Lords can claim superiority. In debates and when scrutinising legislation, the much more independent members of the House of Lords are willing to put forward the interests of minorities to a much greater degree than MPs in the Commons. Many peers have special expertise and experience, qualities that make them uniquely qualified to represent such groups.

Source: original material

In your response you must:
+ compare and contrast the different opinions in the source
+ examine and debate these views in a balanced way
+ analyse and evaluate only the information presented in the source

Answers and quick quiz 6 online

Exam skills

Question 3 above asks you to compare the two chambers in how they fulfil a specific function — in this instance its representative function. It is good practice to use a set of criteria with which to compare the two Houses. We can take the criteria from some of the themes examined in the source itself:
+ the fact that the Commons is elected but the Lords is not
+ representation of minority groups
+ standing up for minority interests

Once the criteria are established, you should consider a rough plan that would help you to analyse the question. A sample plan for the question on representation has been completed in the table below.

Essay plan for the question 'Using the source, evaluate the view that the House of Lords is more representative than the House of Commons.'

Criterion	How it makes the House of Lords less representative than the House of Commons	How it makes the House of Lords more representative than the House of Commons
The fact that the Commons is elected but the Lords is not	Lacks democratic legitimacy	FPTP is deeply unfair and under-represents smaller parties in the House of Commons. Some of these parties have fairer representation in the Lords, especially the Liberal Democrats.
Representation of minority groups	More ethnic minorities and women in the Commons	The numbers aren't hugely different — both Houses could do a better job with regards to resemblance.
Standing up for minority interests	MPs can respond to the needs of constituents.	The Lords has a track record of defending vulnerable sections of the community.

Remember, it is important to decide which arguments are the strongest and why.

Summary

You should now have an understanding of:
+ the structure and composition of the House of Lords and House of Commons
+ the legislative process — how a bill becomes law
+ the different kinds of bills which pass through Parliament, particularly public bills and private members' bills
+ the role of MPs and peers
+ the influence of backbench MPs and the barriers they face
+ the powers of the House of Commons compared to the House of Lords, specifically the limits contained within the Parliament Acts and the Salisbury Convention
+ the role and importance of the opposition
+ the different types of parliamentary questions and an analysis of which ones are more effective with regards to scrutiny
+ parliamentary committees and an analysis of their effectiveness
+ how effectively Parliament performs its legislative, representative and scrutiny functions
+ arguments in favour of and against an elected House of Lords

7 The prime minister and executive

The role of the executive

The UK executive has the following roles:
+ proposing, securing the passage of and implementing legislation
+ proposing a budget and managing the state's finances
+ developing and making policy decisions
+ conducting foreign policy, including relations with other states and international bodies
+ responding to major problems or crises, such as armed conflict, security threats, economic difficulties or social disorder
+ organising and managing the services provided by the state

> **Executive** Also known as 'the government', this is the collective name for the prime minister, cabinet, junior ministers, government departments and their staff.

Remember

The terms 'government' and 'executive' are generally interchangeable, but it is good practice to use the term 'government' when referring to elected ministers and to reserve the use of 'executive' for when you are discussing the wider government, including political advisors and senior civil servants.

The structure of the executive

The structure of the UK executive has the following elements:
+ The prime minister and their close advisors.
+ The cabinet: 20–25 senior ministers appointed by the prime minister.
+ Junior ministers: they tend to run a specific part of a government department.
+ Government departments: of these, the Treasury holds a place of special importance as it controls government finances. Many heads of these departments are members of the cabinet.
+ The senior civil servants who serve government ministers: of these, the cabinet secretary is the most senior. They serve both the prime minister personally and the cabinet collectively.

> **Cabinet** A body of 20–25 senior ministers and other important senior party figures, such as the chief whip, whose meetings are chaired by the prime minister.
>
> **Government department** A part of the executive with a specific responsibility over a policy area.
>
> **Senior civil servants** Officials who give advice to ministers and implement ministers' decisions.
>
> **Cabinet secretary** The most senior civil servant in the UK. The cabinet secretary serves the prime minister and then the cabinet. They organise the work of cabinet and of government at the centre of power.

The prime minister

The office of the prime minister has the following features:
+ The prime minister is the leader of the governing party and so usually commands a majority in the House of Commons.
+ The prime minister is assisted and supported by a large collection of bodies and individuals, which include the cabinet secretary, a chief of staff (often their closest aide), their private office (staffed by senior civil servants), the Number 10 Policy Unit (a group of special advisors) and the Cabinet Office.

> **Cabinet Office** A government department that gives policy advice to the prime minister and cabinet. It is staffed by senior civil servants.

103

The prime minister's main roles are as follows:
+ considered the de facto head of government
+ the government's chief policy maker
+ the nation's chief diplomat
+ appointing the cabinet and chairing its meetings

Now test yourself TESTED

1 Name three individuals or bodies that are part of the executive.
2 Describe two roles of the prime minister.

Answers online

The cabinet

The following are the main features of the UK cabinet:
+ All its members are appointed by the prime minister, who chairs its meetings, normally held once a week, and sets the agenda.
+ It normally numbers 20–25 members.
+ The members are senior government ministers and a few key officials who run the government's business.
+ A few senior party figures may not be cabinet members but still attend meetings. The chief government whip is the best example.
+ Much of the detailed work of cabinet is conducted in cabinet committees. These are small groups of ministers, chaired by the prime minister or another senior cabinet member.
+ Cabinet committees develop policy details and present proposals for the approval of the whole cabinet. In some circumstances, they may be charged with implementing policy.

Cabinet committees Groups established by the prime minister that are able to reduce the burden on the full cabinet by allowing a smaller number of ministers to take decisions on specific policy areas. The membership of these committees is decided by the prime minister.

The cabinet's main functions are:
+ approving policy and settling disputes within government
+ determining the government's reaction to crises and emergencies
+ determining the presentation of government policy

Exam tip

When a question is about power (how powerful is the prime minister, cabinet etc.), it is good practice to consider what the person or institution in question is supposed to do and has the power to do. Then contrast what they are supposed to do with what they are able to do, bringing in some of the limits to their power.

Ministers and their departments

Ministers are ranked into senior and junior posts:
+ Secretary of state: a senior minister who runs a large department and is most likely also to be a cabinet member.
+ Minister of state: they will run a subdivision of the department and will not be a cabinet member. They are often referred to as junior ministers.
+ Parliamentary under-secretary of state: a very junior minister who runs a specialised section of the department.
+ Parliamentary private secretary (PPS): an MP who acts as a link between ministers and MPs. This position is the first rung on the ministerial ladder.

Minister An MP or a peer who takes a position in government, usually in a specific government department.

Collectively, all these ministers are known as the government 'front bench'. All ministers are subject to collective ministerial responsibility (see later section in this chapter).

The roles of ministers and their departments are generally to:

+ draft legislation when it is needed
+ organise the passage of legislation through Parliament and speak in debates on the legislation
+ take decisions as part of the powers they have under secondary legislation
+ answer to Parliament through questions and by appearing in front of select committees

> **Secondary legislation**
> Much of the business of government is conducted using secondary or delegated legislation. These are orders made by ministers which require relatively little parliamentary control. The power to make such orders is given to ministers in primary legislation.

Now test yourself TESTED

3 Describe the difference between a secretary of state and a minister of state.
4 Describe two roles of a minister.

Answers online

Proposing legislation

+ The government engages in consultation by publishing a Green Paper, which sets out a possible course of action or a set of policies, so that MPs, peers and interested parties can make comments and suggest changes.
+ A White Paper is then published, which outlines the specific details of proposed legislation. It is usually published about a year before the legislation is presented to Parliament. Parliament will normally debate the White Paper, and proposed changes may be considered.
+ The party whips check that there is sufficient support for legislation among the governing party's MPs.
+ Legislation will then be formally introduced to Parliament, the process for which is described in Chapter 6.

> **Green Paper** A consultation document (printed on green paper) produced by the government. The aim is to allow those inside and outside Parliament to give feedback on its policy or legislative proposals.
>
> **White Paper** A policy document produced by the government that sets out specific proposals for future legislation. It may include a draft version of a bill that is being planned.

> **Remember**
>
> A large part of the work of the UK executive is taken up with the government's budget. The Treasury, which is led by the chancellor of the exchequer, prepares an annual budget indicating levels of spending, taxes and borrowing. The process also involves allocating funds to government departments, which is negotiated between the Treasury and individual department ministers and approved by cabinet. The House of Commons then has to approve the budget.

Individual ministerial responsibility

Individual ministerial responsibility (IMR) is a constitutional convention. It has four main elements:

1 Ministers must be prepared to be accountable to Parliament for the policies and decisions made by their department. They must answer questions in the House, give evidence before select committees and justify their actions in debate.
2 If a minister makes a serious error of judgement, they should be required to resign. In 2018 the home secretary, Amber Rudd, inadvertently misled Parliament over whether she knew about regional removal targets for illegal immigrants and was forced to resign.
3 If the minister's department makes a serious error, whether or not the minister was involved in the cause of the error, they are likewise bound to resign. Former education secretary Estelle Morris resigned in 2003 after a series of controversies relating to A-level standards and the failure of her department to meet the government's own literacy and numeracy standards.

> **Individual ministerial responsibility** The principle that ministers are responsible for their personal conduct and for the work of their department.

105

4 If a minister's conduct falls below the standards required of someone in public office, they should leave office and may face dismissal by the prime minister. Defence secretary Michael Fallon resigned in October 2017 after revelations of inappropriate behaviour towards women.

The limits to individual ministerial responsibility

REVISED

The convention of IMR has been eroded in recent years:
+ Increasingly, ministers are not taking responsibility for either policy failures of their departments or for their own errors of political judgement.
+ In some instances, ministers are no longer taking responsibility for failings in their personal conduct.

Table 7.1 details some examples of ministers failing to take responsibility for their actions.

Table 7.1 The erosion of individual ministerial responsibility

Type of failure	Example of a minister failing to accept responsibility
If a minister makes a serious error, they should resign.	In 2020 education secretary Gavin Williamson approved an Ofqual algorithm that downgraded A-level results for thousands of students. The policy was eventually reversed, but the education secretary stayed in post.
Ministers should accept responsibility for errors or poor performance by their departments.	In 2019 transport secretary Chris Grayling did not resign after his department awarded a ferry contract for cross-Channel transport in the event of a no-deal Brexit, even though the company that was awarded the contract owned no ferries.
If a minister's personal conduct falls short of what is expected of an elected official, they should leave office.	In 2020 home secretary Priti Patel refused to resign over a Cabinet Office inquiry that uncovered evidence of her bullying civil servants.

Remember

The erosion of IMR has occurred for two main reasons. First, ministerial resignations can make the government look weak and so the government may try to 'ride out the storm' instead. Second, ministers may have shown loyalty to the prime minister and therefore expect a degree of support in return when things go wrong. If the consequence of this is that they are less likely to be sacked, they will feel less pressure to 'jump before they are pushed'.

Now test yourself

TESTED

5 Give three examples where a minister has failed to take individual ministerial responsibility.

6 Give two reasons why the convention of individual ministerial responsibility has been eroded in recent years.

Answers online

Collective ministerial responsibility

Collective ministerial responsibility (CMR) is an unwritten convention of the constitution. The principles of this constitutional convention are as follows:
+ All members of government are jointly responsible for all government policies.

- Ministers should support all government policies in public even if they have private reservations.
- Ministers who oppose a key element of government policy, and who are not prepared to defend it in public, should resign.
- Theresa May saw 17 ministers (four of whom were cabinet members, including Boris Johnson) resign over her Brexit strategy between July 2018 and April 2019.
- If a minister dissents without resigning, they can expect to be dismissed by the prime minister.

> **Collective ministerial responsibility** The convention that ministers must support government decisions in public, regardless of any private reservations. If they are unable to do so, then they should resign.

Collective ministerial responsibility is important for the following reasons:

- It projects a sense of government unity.
- It can help the prime minister maintain their dominant position.
- It stifles dissidence within the government.
- It helps ministers express their reservations privately.
- It can protect individual ministers from pressure if the government takes collective responsibility for a policy.

Table 7.2 describes several important resignations under the doctrine.

Table 7.2 Examples of ministers who refused to take collective ministerial responsibility

Minister	Position	Party	Resignation year	Reason for resignation
Robin Cook	Foreign secretary	Labour	2003	Opposed the government's decision to take part in an invasion of Iraq
Iain Duncan Smith	Work and pensions secretary	Conservative	2016	Disagreed with proposed cuts to disability benefits
Sajid Javid	Chancellor	Conservative	2020	Refused to accept replacement of his advisors with those chosen by the prime minister
Lady Sugg	Junior Foreign Office minister	Conservative	2020	Disagreed with ending the commitment to spend 0.7% of the UK's budget on overseas aid

Limits to collective ministerial responsibility

 REVISED

In recent years, the convention of collective ministerial responsibility has come under strain, with ministers disagreeing with government policy but refusing to resign. The reasons that have limited CMR are outlined in Table 7.3.

Table 7.3 The breakdown in collective ministerial responsibility

Reason	Example
In a coalition, CMR only extends to those policies that the governing parties can agree upon.	During the coalition between the Liberal Democrats and the Conservatives (2010–15), CMR was abandoned for policies where there remained significant disagreement, such as on the renewal of the Trident nuclear missile system.
A specific issue may divide the cabinet.	Divides over Brexit spilled out into the open during Theresa May's tenure as prime minister. Several cabinet ministers criticised her for refusing to take a 'no-deal' Brexit off the table, while others called for a harder stance towards Europe.
Referendums usually involve members of the cabinet campaigning on different sides of the argument.	Five members of David Cameron's cabinet campaigned to leave the EU in the 2016 referendum while the rest campaigned to remain.
A prime minister without sufficient authority may feel unable to dismiss ministers who are disloyal.	Theresa May's failure to secure a majority at the 2017 general election diminished her standing. Cabinet members were said to be 'plotting her downfall' from election night onwards, yet they faced no consequences.
Personality clashes can force cabinet members to choose between two rival camps.	The rivalry between Blair and Brown meant that cabinet members were often labelled as either 'Brownites' or 'Blairites'. Ministers and their aides often leaked details of disagreements, but no one resigned or was sacked over this rivalry.

7 Explain why these ministers refused to accept CMR.

Minister	Why they resigned
Sajid Javid	
Robin Cook	
Lady Sugg	

8 Give three reasons why CMR is important for a prime minister.

Answers online

Exam tip

You can use your knowledge of collective ministerial responsibility in a wider question regarding prime ministerial power. A cabinet that maintains CMR gives an impression of unity, which in turn strengthens the prime minister's authority. In contrast, if a government suffers a number of resignations it will lead to the erosion of the prime minister's authority.

The powers of the prime minister

The prime minister derives their authority and dominance of government from the following sources of power:

+ patronage
+ royal prerogative
+ parliamentary majority
+ party support
+ personal mandate

The following sections explain these powers and consider how they help the prime minister increase their authority. The limitations of these powers will also be covered.

Patronage and the appointment of ministers

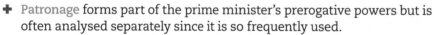

REVISED ⬤

+ Patronage forms part of the prime minister's prerogative powers but is often analysed separately since it is so frequently used.
+ The main component of this power is the ability to appoint and dismiss cabinet and junior ministers (the co-called payroll vote).
+ Members of the cabinet therefore owe their promotion to the prime minister and are bound by collective ministerial responsibility.
+ Prime ministers also have a say in other public appointments, including those of the most senior civil servants.

The power of patronage allows the prime minister the following advantages:

+ It enables the prime minister to shape the ideological direction of the cabinet. Thatcher appointed 'Dries', New Right Tories who agreed with her policies.
+ It means the prime minister can reward those who are loyal to them. Boris Johnson promoted those who supported his leadership campaign (e.g. Rishi Sunak) and sacked those who questioned his Brexit policy (e.g. Julian Smith).
+ It gives the prime minister the opportunity to promote younger MPs with potential and to increase diversity. Theresa May promoted younger women to senior positions, such as Amber Rudd to home secretary.

> **Patronage** The power of appointment and dismissal. In relation to the prime minister, patronage over ministerial offices gives them great power because it promotes loyalty among those who are promoted or who hope to be promoted.
>
> **Payroll vote** Senior ministers and junior ministers who, since they owe their promotion to the prime minister, can be relied upon to vote in favour of government legislation.

Factors governing the selection of ministers

Prime ministers have to take into account a range of factors when selecting ministers and therefore their powers of patronage are not absolute. Table 7.4 details the constraints upon their power of patronage.

Table 7.4 Constraints upon the power of patronage

Factor	Example
The prime minister often has to satisfy the various factions within their political party.	Thatcher initially was forced into appointing the 'Wets', moderates who disagreed with her New Right agenda.
It is safer to have potential rivals in cabinet, bound under collective ministerial responsibility, than to have them 'sniping' from the backbenches.	Both Cameron and May felt it was safer to have Boris Johnson in their cabinets than as a backbench MP.
The type of government also affects the leeway with patronage.	In a coalition, the prime minister is forced to promote MPs from the junior coalition partner. Cameron agreed to appoint five Lib Dems to cabinet. With a small majority and then a hung parliament, Theresa May had to promote prominent 'Brexiteers', including Johnson, Liam Fox and David Davis, to senior positions.
Ministers may refuse a job.	Theresa May's attempts to reshuffle unfavourable ministers seriously backfired in January 2018 when Jeremy Hunt refused to move from his post as health secretary.

Making links

When referring to the limits of patronage, you should incorporate the need for prime ministers to reflect the ideological factions of their party. For example, Blair had to consider those who favoured traditional socialism while Thatcher had to initially promote One Nation Conservatives.

The royal prerogative

REVISED

The royal prerogative concerns those powers that have passed from the monarch to the prime minister. Their use has not in the past required approval by Parliament and thus they have allowed the prime minister to act independently. Table 7.5 explains what the royal prerogative allows the prime minister to do and how it has been limited in recent years.

> **Royal prerogative** The unwritten powers that have passed from the monarch to the prime minister. These include powers of patronage, acting as commander-in-chief and negotiating foreign treaties.

Table 7.5 The powers and limitations of the royal prerogative

What the royal prerogative allows the prime minister to do	Recent limits to the royal prerogative
The prime minister is considered the de facto commander-in-chief of the armed forces. Theresa May authorised bombing of Syria in 2018 without a vote in the House of Commons.	It is now accepted that the prime minister should make major military commitments only 'on the advice and with the sanction of Parliament'. A precedent was set, in the vote on the Iraq War, that Parliament, not the prime minister, has the final say on committing ground troops into military conflict.
The prime minister is effectively chief diplomat since they are able to sign treaties and enter into negotiation with other countries. After the 2016 referendum, successive prime ministers took the lead in negotiating a post-Brexit relationship with the EU.	Treaties that have been approved by Parliament can only be undone by Parliament, a fact confirmed by the UK Supreme Court's decisions relating to Brexit.
The prime minister has huge influence in deciding the date of the next election, capitalising on favourable circumstances, as they can ask the monarch to dissolve Parliament. Thatcher called an election in 1983 to capitalise on her popularity after the Falklands War.	The Fixed-term Parliaments Act requires the prime minister to win a supermajority in Parliament for an election to be called early. While Boris Johnson was able eventually to hold an election in December 2019, the House of Commons initially blocked him from calling an election earlier on in that year.

Now test yourself   TESTED ⬤

9   Identify three constraints on the prime minister's power to appoint their cabinet.

10 Explain three ways in which the royal prerogative has been weakened in recent years.

Answers online

Parliamentary majority

REVISED ⬤

A prime minister, as leader of the largest party in the House of Commons, usually enjoys a Commons majority. Having a parliamentary majority will increase the likelihood that the government's legislative agenda will be passed.

However, the size of majority changes from election to election and a prime minister who lacks a sizeable Commons majority will have far greater difficulty in achieving their aims. Table 7.6 exemplifies the consequences for prime ministers who did and did not have large Commons majorities.

Table 7.6 The effect of majorities on prime ministers' ability to achieve their legislative agendas

Prime ministers with Commons majorities	Prime ministers without large Commons majorities
After landslide election victories in 1997 and 2001, Tony Blair did not suffer a single Commons defeat between 1997 and 2005.	The halving of the Blair government's Commons majority at the 2005 general election resulted in its first Commons defeat in 2006, when proposals on detaining terror suspects for up to 90 days were rejected.
Having won a majority after the 2015 general election, the Conservatives were able to pass laws they had been unable to pass in coalition, notably legislation paving the way to a referendum on EU membership.	With just a small Commons majority after 2015, the Tories lost a vote on loosening Sunday trading laws in March 2016.
Boris Johnson's 80-seat parliamentary majority secured at the 2019 general election allowed him to steer through Brexit at the end of January 2020.	In contrast, Theresa May was unable to steer through her Brexit legislation after failing to win a Commons majority at the 2017 general election, suffering the heaviest Commons defeat of any British prime minister when MPs rejected her Brexit bill by 230 votes in January 2019.

Remember

Even prime ministers with large Commons majorities may be limited in the laws they are able to pass. If they sense that they could face a large rebellion among their own MPs, or if they feel they may lose, a vote might be pulled or changes might be made to the bill in order to win over wavering MPs.

Party support

REVISED ⬤

The prime minister can usually count upon the support of their party. To that end, they can use party whips to instill discipline and remove the whip from MPs who are disloyal. However, prime ministers can never take the support of their party for granted and those who do normally face a backlash or are even forced to resign. Table 7.7 gives examples of prime ministers who benefited from general party support and instances of when they lacked it.

Table 7.7 Prime ministers and the support of their parties

Examples of party support for prime ministers	Examples of when prime ministers have lacked party support
After securing huge parliamentary majorities at the 1983 and 1987 general elections, most Conservative MPs united around Thatcher's privatisation programme.	Splits over Europe and the introduction of the poll tax led to Thatcher's resignation in November 1990, following a leadership contest that, after the first round of counting, indicated a lack of support among Tory backbenchers.
Despite Gordon Brown's unpopularity as prime minister between 2007 and 2010, not a single Labour Party MP made an official attempt to hold a leadership contest.	Brown still had few MPs willing to energetically defend him in the press.
Despite the Remain/Leave divide in the Tory Party, only one Tory MP (Ken Clarke) voted against triggering Article 50, the mechanism by which the UK informed the EU of its intention to leave.	Theresa May accepted that she would step down as prime minister after the Brexit process was completed, a price she had to pay for surviving a motion of no confidence as party leader in December 2018.
Boris Johnson removed the whip of several Remain-supporting MPs and at the 2019 general election those MPs were replaced by pro-Brexit candidates. Subsequently, not a single Conservative MP voted against the EU Withdrawal Agreement Act 2020.	Boris Johnson's Conservative Party remains divided over the size of government, with neo-liberals fearing increases in spending and One Nation Conservatives in the 'red wall' seats that were won from Labour in 2019 calling for public investment.

> **Exam tip**
>
> It is best practice to use examples of a number of prime ministers in your essays. As a minimum, try to refer to at least one prime minister before 1997 and one prime minister after 1997.

Personal mandate

The prime minister's personal qualities may bolster their authority and their ability to dominate government and Parliament. Furthermore, if they win a general election, they often claim authority to introduce the policies they care most about or to force through reforms that might be unpopular within their own party. Conversely, a prime minister who lacks charisma and gravitas, or who is not seen as a 'winner', will find their authority much reduced. Table 7.8 gives examples of prime ministers who were able to claim and use their personal mandate and others who found it less easy to do so.

> **Personal mandate** The individual authority claimed by prime ministers to steer the policy direction of government, largely as a result of their popularity, recent election victories and personal attributes.

Table 7.8 Prime ministers and their personal mandate

Prime ministers who were able to claim a personal mandate	Prime ministers who struggled to claim a personal mandate
Tony Blair's skyrocketing approval ratings in the early years of his premiership gave him greater authority in Parliament to enact controversial public-sector reforms that were opposed by many within his own party.	Gordon Brown succeeded Tony Blair without a leadership contest or a general election, limiting his legitimacy in the eyes of the public.
David Cameron consistently polled more favourably than his own party, allowing him to introduce policies that were close to his heart, most notably his Big Society programme and National Citizen Service.	Theresa May was accused of lacking empathy when she initially failed to meet residents of Grenfell Tower after the building had caught fire in June 2017.

> **Remember**
>
> The qualities that increase the appeal and authority of a prime minister could be seen as a double-edged sword. Cameron and Blair were seen by some as comfortable in the media spotlight but by others as lacking in sincerity, as 'too smooth' and thus dishonest.

> **Making links**
>
> When referring to a prime minister's personal mandate, refer to valence issues from the voting behaviour topic in Paper 1, and how trust in a party leader can help them not only to win elections but also to govern.

7 The prime minister and executive

My Revision Notes: Pearson Edexcel A-Level Politics: UK politics second edition

11 Complete the table below by explaining how each source of power can help the prime minister.

Source of power	How it can help the prime minister
Having a parliamentary majority	
Party support	
Personal mandate	

Answers online

The relationship between the prime minister and the cabinet

Cabinet government

REVISED

Traditionally, the UK government has been described as a cabinet government, which consisted of the following features:
+ The cabinet was viewed as the central decision-making body.
+ Any disputes within the government would be resolved in the cabinet.
+ For a policy to become 'official government policy', the cabinet would have to approve it.
+ The prime minister was considered *primus inter pares*.
+ The prime minister enjoyed a higher status than their colleagues but could not make decisions without them.

However, there has been a shift from the 1960s onwards towards a prime ministerial government, which consists of the following features:
+ The prime minister controls the agenda of cabinet meetings.
+ Prime ministers use the media, not just Parliament and the cabinet, to get messages across to the public.
+ The cabinet is packed with the prime minister's supporters.
+ The prime minister makes greater use of their royal prerogative powers, particularly with regard to foreign relations — foreign policy is conducted by the prime minister and not by the cabinet.

Cabinet government A system of government where the cabinet is the central policy-making body.

Primus inter pares A Latin term meaning 'first among equals'. It is applied to the prime minister, seen as the most important member of the cabinet but not one who is domineering.

Prime ministerial government Political circumstances in which the prime minister dominates policy making and the whole machinery of government.

The powers and significance of the cabinet

REVISED

When considering the debate about the power of the cabinet, it is necessary to examine the numerous governmental functions it is supposed to carry out and whether it continues to do so, or whether those functions are now carried out by the prime minister or by government departments instead. Table 7.9 considers the debate about the continued role of the cabinet in carrying out the work of government.

Table 7.9 The importance of the cabinet

Governmental function	The role of the cabinet	How these functions are carried out elsewhere
Policy formulation	The cabinet often sets out the government's general principles over what legislation should contain.	Detailed work on individual policy is carried out in smaller groups. The ban on smoking in pubs was debated in cabinet, but the actual wording of the text was drafted by the Department of Health.
Dealing with crisis	The cabinet often meets during difficult periods to present a 'show of unity' and to agree a way forward. After Black Wednesday (when interest rates rocketed in 1992), the cabinet met to agree economic policy.	In a crisis, the prime minister often relies on small teams of experts and advisors, or upon **COBRA (COBR)**. During the Iraq War, Blair relied on just a few ministers, including Geoff Hoon (defence secretary) and Jack Straw (foreign secretary).
Controlling the parliamentary agenda	The cabinet can be the forum whereby ministers compete to win parliamentary time for the legislation their departments wish to pass.	Decisions on which legislation to prioritise are made elsewhere. In the 2010–15 coalition, the **'quad'** met each week to discuss Liberal Democrat and Conservative priorities.
Approving decisions made elsewhere	Cabinet is an 'endorsing body', approving policies formulated elsewhere (such as in small cabinet committees).	The prime minister can establish cabinet committees, which discuss, propose and, in some instances, decide policy. Boris Johnson created various Covid-19 committees that were tasked with implementing policies relating to health, economic matters and public services.
Settling disputes	The cabinet allows secretaries of state to advocate for their policy positions and to compromise where necessary. The decision to scrap the Educational Maintenance Allowance for sixth-form students was only agreed upon once senior Liberal Democrat cabinet members in the 2010–2015 coalition secured extra funding for its replacement.	Most disputes are resolved elsewhere, usually involving bilateral meetings between individual cabinet members and the prime minister. In 2017 Theresa May and her chancellor Philip Hammond held tense discussions over whether to scrap the planned rise in national insurance contributions.

COBRA (COBR) The Civil Contingencies Committee convened to handle matters of national emergency or major disruption. Its membership varies according to the situation, but it is often chaired by the prime minister, and is attended by senior ministers chosen from relevant government departments and those with specific expertise in the matter at hand.

The **'quad'** An arrangement specifically created for the coalition government between 2010 and 2015, whereby two senior Conservatives (David Cameron, George Osborne) and two senior Liberal Democrats (Nick Clegg, Danny Alexander) would meet to decide government policy.

Now test yourself

TESTED

12 Explain three features of cabinet government.

13 Explain three features of prime ministerial government.

Answers online

Exam tip

It is generally a good idea to allow 45 minutes to complete a 30-mark question. However, to build up to this, practise writing a paragraph in 10 minutes. Further advice on structuring paragraphs can be found at the end of this chapter.

Circumstances that affect the power of the cabinet

The power of the cabinet is directly affected by the power and authority of the prime minister. A prime minister who is popular and who has a strong majority in the House of Commons is able to have a greater influence over policy and decision making than the cabinet. However, weaker prime ministers who lack popular appeal and who have slim majorities are often challenged by rivals in cabinet. Table 7.10 considers the circumstances that may increase or limit the power of the cabinet.

Table 7.10 Circumstances that affect the power of the cabinet

Circumstance	How it may limit the power of the cabinet	How it may increase the power of cabinet
Size of majority	Prime ministers with large majorities will feel that they can disregard their cabinets, safe in the knowledge that there are plenty of backbenchers to vote for their policies and accept promotions should cabinet members resign. Tony Blair and his chancellor Gordon Brown announced the policy of Bank of England independence without prior consultation with the cabinet.	A prime minister whose party lacks a large majority or who fails to have one will need the support of their cabinet to stay in their job. John Major was forced to negotiate opt-outs on specific sections of the Maastricht Treaty to appease eurosceptics in his cabinet who feared further EU integration.
Prime ministerial preference	Some prime ministers prefer to bully or cajole cabinet members into accepting their ideas, and some are also secretive and prefer making decisions with their advisors. Theresa May allowed her two closest advisors, Fiona Hill and Nick Timothy, to write large parts of the 2017 Conservative Party manifesto, rather than having an open dialogue with cabinet.	Some prime ministers prefer to consult cabinet colleagues and delegate decision making. David Cameron gave education secretary Michael Gove a free hand in setting education policy.
Characters within cabinet	Prime ministers use their patronage powers to ensure the cabinet is loyal to them. Johnson only promoted MPs to the cabinet who agreed with his Brexit policy.	Senior cabinet members or the so-called 'big beasts' may influence promotions to the cabinet. Blair had to accept an increasing number of MPs who were 'Brownites' instead of 'Blairites', in order to satisfy chancellor Gordon Brown, a 'big beast' in the Blair cabinet.
The issue and its importance	The cabinet will likely be consulted far more when difficult decisions have to be made on important issues. Gordon Brown's scrapping of the 10p tax-band rate was discussed at length in cabinet because some cabinet members threatened privately to resign.	Issues of secondary importance will be left to the prime minister. Despite cabinet concerns, Blair pushed ahead with the construction of the Millennium Dome. The issue was not seen by cabinet members as important enough to resign over.

Revision activity

Make sure you can:

1 list the functions of the cabinet

2 explain the circumstances that increase and decrease the power and influence of the cabinet

Is the prime minister effectively a president?

In order to consider this question, it is first important to distinguish between a parliamentary government and a presidential government. Table 7.11 compares the two different systems.

Table 7.11 Features of parliamentary and presidential government

Parliamentary government	Presidential government
The executive is formed from the legislature, which means that members of the House of Commons and House of Lords make up the government. This arrangement is called the fusion of powers (see Chapter 5).	There is a strict separation of personnel (separation of powers). Members of the legislature cannot also be members of the executive.
The government cannot take action without the approval of Parliament. It is constrained by parliamentary sovereignty.	A president executes the law and is not constrained by the sovereignty of the legislature.
Scrutiny of the executive takes place inside Parliament, through parliamentary questions on the floor of the two chambers or in the various committees.	The president cannot be summoned by the legislature. Scrutiny takes place as much outside the legislature through the media as it does inside of it.
A prime minister is reliant on their parliamentary majority and their cabinet for their position and support.	A president relies on the advice of their advisors but can choose to largely ignore their cabinet.
There is no direct election for prime minister. They are elected as an MP like every other member of the House of Commons.	The president is directly elected and enjoys a separate mandate from those elected to the legislature.

As is clear from Table 7.11, there is undoubtedly a parliamentary system of government in operation in the UK. This prevents prime ministers from being true presidents. Yet some prime ministers have adopted different aspects of a presidential government or presidential style. Table 7.12 considers in more detail the argument over whether prime ministers are effectively presidents.

Table 7.12 The debate on presidentialism and presidential style

How prime ministers have sought to act as presidents	Limits to prime ministers' ability to act as presidents
Election campaigns have become personalised, with prime ministers the focal point. Theresa May made the 2017 general election about her 'strong and stable leadership'.	Personalised election campaigns damage the credibility of leaders if they lack campaigning skills and popular support. Public faith in Theresa May's claim to be 'strong and stable' was weakened after the U-turn on the party's policy on health and social care (dubbed the 'dementia tax').
Prime ministers increasingly create strategic space between themselves and other institutions, including the cabinet, Parliament and their own party. This style is often referred to as spatial leadership. Cameron painted himself as a 'moderniser', out to reform his stuffy party by advocating policies such as legalising gay marriage.	Spatial leadership is not possible due to the fusion of powers; prime ministers are 'reined in' by the forces of constraint. Theresa May lost control of the payroll vote, accepting in March 2019 that junior ministers could vote with their consciences on the indicative vote process over Brexit.
Prime ministers are increasingly reliant upon their advisors, similar to a US president. In his first year as prime minister, Boris Johnson allowed senior advisor Dominic Cummings huge influence over the machinery of government.	Over-reliance on advisors can damage the credibility of prime ministers. After the poorly received manifesto and the loss of majority after the 2017 general election, Theresa May was forced to sack senior advisors Nick Timothy and Fiona Hill.
Prime ministers seek to act independently of Parliament in foreign affairs, similarly to how a US president takes action without the US Congress. Theresa May's use of the royal prerogative in the 2018 Syria bombings highlighted her preference to act separately from Parliament.	Since the Iraq War, Parliament has become far more assertive. In 2013 David Cameron failed to persuade Parliament to vote in favour of military action against the Assad regime in Syria.

14 Look at the following descriptions. Are aspects of a parliamentary or presidential government being described?

Description	Parliamentary or presidential?
The executive is formed from the legislature.	
The leader is directly elected and enjoys a separate mandate from those in the legislature.	
The leader relies on advisors rather than other politicians.	
The leader seeks to act independently of the legislature.	
Scrutiny of the executive predominantly takes place within the legislature.	

Answers online

Presidential government
A system where the legislature and executive are separate from each other and where the leader is directly elected.

Spatial leadership The attempt by prime ministers to be seen above politics as the nation's leader, by separating themselves or 'taking on' institutions, their cabinet and/or their party.

Prime ministerial profiles

The following four profiles can be used as evidence in assessing prime ministerial power. The particular circumstances of each prime minister are described.

Margaret Thatcher

In office: 1979–90

Majorities: 1979: 43, 1983: 144, 1987: 102

Description of political stance: neo-liberal and neo-conservative

Circumstances that increased her power:
+ Decisive parliamentary majorities.
+ Good image in a high proportion of the press.
+ Good public image among the middle classes.
+ Reputation for strength in foreign policy.
+ Respected by foreign leaders.
+ After 1983, led an ideologically united party.
+ Hailed a national hero following the success of the war to liberate the Falkland Islands from Argentinian occupation.
+ There was an economic boom in the mid-1980s.
+ Strongly backed by cabinet after 1983.

Circumstances that limited her power:
+ Poor public image among the working classes.
+ Liberal and left-wing media criticised her heavily.
+ Obstinacy in pushing the unpopular poll tax policy led to her downfall.
+ In her latter years the economic situation began to deteriorate.
+ A small moderate group in the party opposed her implacably.

Circumstances of her downfall:

Thatcher refused to drop her support for the introduction of an unpopular form of local taxation known as the poll tax. When it was feared that the party would be defeated at the 1992 general election, a leadership challenge was mounted and Thatcher was replaced by John Major in 1990.

Tony Blair

In office: 1997–2007

Majorities: 1997: 179, 2001: 167, 2005: 66

Description of political stance: moderate social democrat (Third Way or New Labour)

Circumstances that increased his power:
+ Decisive parliamentary majorities.
+ Good image in a high proportion of the press up to 2003.
+ Charismatic public image among both the working and middle classes until 2003.
+ Positive image abroad until the Iraq War in 2003.
+ There was an economic boom in the later 1990s.
+ Respected by foreign leaders.
+ Led an ideologically united party.

Circumstances that limited his power:
+ Public image became tarnished in later years.
+ After 2003 faced strong opposition from the well-supported Gordon Brown.
+ The Iraq War proved to be a disaster for his reputation.

Circumstances of his downfall:

Blair's reputation declined after the Iraq War. Increasing numbers of Labour members wanted to see Gordon Brown as their leader. Pressure built up as Brown became more popular. Blair resigned in 2007 in favour of Brown.

David Cameron

In office: 2010–16

Majorities: 2010: no majority, 2015: 12

Description of political stance: socially liberal; New Right economic policy

Circumstances that increased his power:
+ Supported by the press and comfortable in the media spotlight.
+ Few rivals in cabinet; enjoyed a close working relationship with chancellor George Osborne.
+ Opposition Labour Party was weak and increasingly disunited.

Circumstances that limited his power:
+ Forced into coalition government in 2010. This severely reduced his control over government.
+ Won only a very narrow parliamentary majority in 2015.
+ Constantly faced opposition from right-wing eurosceptics within his own party.
+ Introduced a programme of severe and increasingly unpopular economic austerity.

Circumstances of his downfall:

As a result of pressure from his own party and the rise of UKIP, Cameron was forced to promise a referendum on UK membership of the EU in 2016. When the outcome was to leave the EU after he had campaigned strongly to remain, he resigned.

My Revision Notes: Pearson Edexcel A-Level Politics: UK politics second edition

Boris Johnson

In office: 2019–

Majorities: July-November 2019 no majority, December 2019: 80

Description of political stance: mix of one nation conservative on economic policy and New Right policies on Brexit and immigration

Circumstances that increased his power:
+ Gained a reputation for winning elections and referendums.
+ Won a personal mandate to 'get Brexit done'.
+ Had a loyal cabinet in first year in office.

Circumstances that limited his power:
+ Was seen as too reliant on close advisor Dominic Cummings.
+ The Covid-19 pandemic consumed the government's agenda.
+ Criticised for several policy U-turns, including the provision of free school meals during the summer holidays.
+ Divisions in the party have emerged over levels of public spending.

Now test yourself

TESTED ◯

15 For each description in the table, identify the prime minister and give the details that fit.

Description	Prime minister	Details
Resigned after losing a referendum vote		
Resigned in favour of a rival from within their own party		
Resigned due to pressure from the cabinet		

Answers online

Exam practice

1 Evaluate the view that cabinet government is dead. [30]

2 Evaluate the view that the prime minister dominates the UK political system. [30]

3 Using the source, evaluate the view that the prime minister is now effectively a president. [30]

> The distinctions between UK prime ministers and US presidents are less easy to make nowadays, since a number of recent prime ministers have adopted aspects of a presidential style. They have attempted to separate themselves from their cabinet, often by claiming a personal mandate if, as was the case with Margaret Thatcher and Tony Blair, they had won large parliamentary majorities. These prime ministers were as comfortable 'taking on' their own party as they were the opposition. Furthermore, leaders such as Theresa May and Boris Johnson have relied heavily upon close advisors, in a similar way to US presidents. Prime ministers have also attempted to act separately from Parliament, taking a greater interest in foreign affairs than have prime ministers in the past.
>
> However, while prime ministers might seek to stretch their independence from the cabinet and from Parliament, the forces of constraint will ensure that they will be limited in their ability to do so. The UK retains a parliamentary system of government whereby the prime minister is not directly elected. Those leaders without a strong parliamentary majority are unable to separate themselves from the legislature and have to work hard to secure a majority for every vote. Even if prime ministers enjoy a comfortable majority, they ignore cabinet at their peril. Margaret Thatcher found this out to her cost and so too have many other prime ministers. It is therefore clear that adopting a 'presidential style' is hardly the same as being an actual president.
>
> Source: original material

In your response you must:
+ compare and contrast the different opinions in the source
+ examine and debate these views in a balanced way
+ analyse and evaluate only the information presented in the source

Answers and quick quiz 7 online

Exam skills

It is important to try to meet all the assessment objectives (AOs) in every single paragraph. Here is a brief reminder of what these assessment objectives are:

+ AO1: Knowledge and understanding (arguments, key terms and examples)
+ AO2: Analysis (having a balanced argument and explaining why the arguments are relevant)
+ AO3: Evaluation (deciding between stronger and weaker arguments)

The table below provides a paragraph template that should help you to meet these assessment objectives.

Step	What to do	Sentence starters that might help you	AO met
1	Introduce an argument that is unconvincing or weak.	'There are those who mistakenly claim that…'	AO3
2	Develop this argument with examples.	'They may point to…'	AO1
3	Explain why this example or argument is relevant to the question.	'This argument is relevant to the question because…'	AO2
4	Give reasons as to why this argument is weak.	'However, this argument lacks merit because…'	AO3
5	Introduce an argument that is more convincing or stronger.	'The more convincing argument is that…'	AO3
6	Develop this argument with examples.	'For instance,…'	AO1
7	Explain why this argument is stronger than the argument mentioned at the start of the paragraph.	'This argument is ultimately stronger because…'	AO2, AO3

Summary

You should now have an understanding of:
+ the role and structure of the executive
+ individual ministerial responsibility and its limits
+ collective ministerial responsibility and how its erosion affects the authority of the prime minister
+ the sources of prime ministerial power, specifically patronage, the royal prerogative, parliamentary majority, party support and personal mandate

+ the limits to these powers
+ cabinet and prime ministerial government
+ the debate about the importance of the cabinet
+ the debate about whether prime ministers are now effectively presidents

8 Relations between branches

The branches of government consist of the following:
+ the legislature (Parliament)
+ the executive (government)
+ the judiciary

The role of the judiciary

The role of the judiciary can be summarised as follows:
+ **Dispensing justice:** hearing criminal cases and civil disputes.
+ **Interpreting law:** when the meaning and application of law are unclear, it is the role of judges to interpret its true meaning.
+ **Establishing case law:** judges decide how the law is to be applied in particular kinds of case. Once established, other courts follow the same case law.
+ **Making law** through declaring common law: not all law is developed by Parliament; some is made by judges when they declare what the law should be as we commonly understand it. When courts perform this role, they set judicial precedent.
+ Judicial review: The power to review actions of government or other bodies such as local authorities and decide whether those actions are lawful.
+ **Public inquiries:** judges sometimes hold inquiries into matters of major public concern and recommend action to government and Parliament.

> **Judicial precedent** A legal principle that when a court makes a particular interpretation of the meaning of law or a judgment about how the law should be applied in a specific case, that interpretation must be followed by all courts in subsequent cases. Only a higher court can overturn a judicial precedent.
>
> **Judicial review** The power to declare actions of government or other bodies such as local authorities as *ultra vires* or acting beyond their power given to them in law.

> **Judiciary** A general term referring to the whole legal system. In terms of politics, the senior judiciary are those judges and courts that make decisions of wider political significance.

> **Common law** Unwritten law that can be declared valid by a court on the grounds that certain rules have existed for a long time and are generally accepted by people as law. Common law often concerns the rights that citizens enjoy. Such law is passed down through judicial precedents.

The Supreme Court

The key features of the Supreme Court are as follows:
+ It is the highest court in the UK.
+ Only the UK Parliament can overturn decisions of the Supreme Court by passing new legislation or amending existing law.

The membership of the court is as follows:
+ There are 12 senior judges who all have extensive legal experience.
+ The head of the court is the president of the Supreme Court.
+ The judges are appointed by an independent panel of the country's senior legal figures, so that it can be independent of political pressure.

The role of the Supreme Court can be described as follows:
+ It is the final court of appeal for all civil cases in the UK and criminal cases from England, Wales and Northern Ireland.
+ It concentrates on cases of the greatest public and constitutional importance.
+ It may hear constitutional law cases, as well as criminal and civil law cases.
+ It hears appeals on arguable points of law — it clarifies the meaning and application of law which may not be clear from the wording of the law.

> **Supreme Court** The highest court in the UK political system.
>
> **Constitutional law** Statute laws, common law or conventional rules which concern the ways in which government operates and which deal with the distribution of political power.
>
> **Civil law** Unlike criminal law, which involves criminal activity, civil law refers to private disputes between individuals and organisations.

> **Remember**
>
> The US Supreme Court has more power than the UK Supreme Court because it is able to interpret the USA's codified constitution.

Answers and quick quizzes at **www.hoddereducation.co.uk/myrevisionnotesdownloads**

Table 8.1 outlines some key cases to illustrate the work of the Supreme Court.

Table 8.1 Important UK Supreme Court rulings

Case	Year	Legal or constitutional principle	Issue	Outcome
Schindler v *Duchy of Lancaster*	2016	The right to vote	Should UK citizens who had lived abroad for more than 15 years be able to vote in the 2016 EU referendum?	The vote was denied to such citizens as they had forfeited their rights by living abroad for so long.
Miller	2017	The prime minister's prerogative powers over treaties and diplomacy	The case challenged the prime minister's claim that they could automatically trigger Article 50 of the Lisbon Treaty, the provision by which an EU member state signals its intention to leave the EU.	The court ruled that only Parliament could give the prime minister authority to trigger article 50 — their prerogative powers could not undermine parliamentary sovereignty.
Miller II	2019	The prime minister's prerogative powers to prorogue (suspend) Parliament	The prime minister advised the monarch to suspend Parliament, which is usually a formality after a year or so, paving the way for a short recess and then the next parliamentary session. However, did he do so to avoid scrutiny over his Brexit plans?	The court ruled that Boris Johnson's advice to the monarch had on this occasion been unlawful, since it was given with intention to evade parliamentary scrutiny.
Friends of the Earth v *Heathrow Airport*	2020	Judicial review	Whether the government ignored the UK's climate change commitments under the Paris Agreement by giving the go-ahead for a third runway at Heathrow Airport.	Construction of a third runway at Heathrow could proceed, as the government was still taking into account its legal obligations on the environment.

Now test yourself   TESTED ⬤

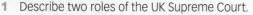

1 Describe two roles of the UK Supreme Court.
2 Describe two Supreme Court cases that appear to have limited the prime minister's royal prerogative.

Answers online

Exam tip

It is essential that you can explain a number of key legal cases to illustrate any answers concerning the role and power of the judiciary.

Judicial neutrality

The neutrality of the whole judiciary (judicial neutrality), including the Supreme Court, is a key principle. It implies the following:
+ Judges should show no political bias.
+ Judges should not show any bias in favour of, or against, any section of society.
+ Judges should base their judgments purely on the principles of law and justice and not on the basis of their own prejudices.
+ As judges have security of tenure, they cannot be dismissed on the basis of their judgments.

Judicial neutrality The principle that judges should not be influenced by their personal opinions and that they should remain outside of party politics.

Security of tenure Judges are effectively appointed for life or until a fixed retirement age, subject to proper behaviour. They cannot be removed for a decision that the government dislikes.

Judicial independence

Judicial independence is a key principle of a democracy. It is important for a number of reasons:
+ Judges need to be able to enforce the rule of law (equality under the law) without any external pressure.

Judicial independence The principle that the judiciary should be free of political interference and criticism, particularly from the executive.

121

+ Judges hear cases of political importance involving the government itself, so they must not be subject to pressure from government if they are to give a neutral judgment.
+ Judges must be able to protect the rights of citizens without fear of retribution if they defy government wishes.
+ The judiciary is, in some cases, a key check on executive power.

Judicial independence is upheld in a number of ways:
+ Judges are appointed for life, so they cannot be dismissed if the government disagrees with their judgments.
+ Judges cannot have their incomes threatened if they make decisions against government wishes.
+ Judges are appointed by a commission which is independent of government.
+ It is the duty of government to protect judges from external pressure, for example from media criticism.

Table 8.2 considers how far the judiciary can be seen as independent and neutral.

Table 8.2 The debate on judicial independence and neutrality

The judiciary is independent and neutral	Limits to judicial independence and neutrality
Judges are all experienced courtroom lawyers who are used to serving the law and the rule of law in a neutral fashion, rather than in a biased way.	The lack of social diversity in the senior judiciary has led to charges that the courts are unconsciously biased against certain groups, particularly those groups who often feel most let down by the criminal justice system — women and those from minority ethnic communities.
Since the Constitutional Reform Act (2005), an independent Judicial Appointments Commission (JAC) recommends candidates for judicial appointments on a more transparent basis, free from political interference.	There is still some political input into senior appointments, despite the creation of the JAC. Formal selection responsibility continues to reside with the lord chancellor, who is appointed by the prime minister, and who may reject the first-choice candidate suggested by the JAC.
The creation of the UK Supreme Court resulted in the physical separation between the legislature and the judiciary, since the court resides in a separate building.	It is argued that the creation of the Supreme Court was only a 'cosmetic' exercise. Indeed, the Supreme Court's powers are largely only the same as those of the Law Lords, making it still limited in its ability to hold the government to account, a key tenet of judicial independence.
The so-called *sub judice* rule in both houses of Parliament prevents MPs and peers from discussing a current or impending court case.	MPs and the media openly question Supreme Court decisions. The *Daily Mail* ran a headline claiming the Supreme Court judges were 'enemies of the people' over the court decisions relating to Brexit. Some claim this kind of exposure could prevent the court from taking tough decisions in the future, limiting its independence.
Judges have openly criticised government decisions. In 2014 the lord chief justice of England and Wales condemned an attempt by government to hold a completely secret trial under the 2013 Justice and Security Act.	In criticising the government, judges may well be acting independently but in doing so are not necessarily acting neutrally.
The decisions relating to Brexit show a willingness to take on the government, demonstrating independence. The 2019 prorogation case denied the prime minister the right to prorogue (suspend) Parliament for a lengthy amount of time without a vote.	Parliament can limit the power and thus the independence of the judiciary. The 2019 Conservative manifesto promised to 'review' the powers of the Supreme Court, which was arguably included as a direct response to the court's rulings pertaining to Brexit.

Making links

When referring to the Supreme Court's decisions relating to Brexit, mention also the EU referendum of 2016.

The Supreme Court and the protection of rights

Table 8.3 considers the effectiveness of the UK Supreme Court in protecting rights.

Table 8.3 The effectiveness of the Supreme Court in protecting rights

How the Supreme Court can protect rights	Limits on the Supreme Court's ability to protect rights
The Supreme Court can use incompatibility statements given to it under the Human Rights Act to rule that proposed laws are in breach of the Human Rights Act.	Incompatibility statements are not binding upon Parliament.
The Supreme Court can interpret the European Convention on Human Rights (ECHR). Example: the Brewster case (2017) confirmed that cohabiting couples enjoyed the same pension rights as married couples under the ECHR.	The UK Supreme Court has no enforcement power. Environmental groups have claimed that the government has failed to respond fast enough to court rulings that found the government breached air quality laws that affect the health rights of citizens.
The Supreme Court enforces the rule of law. Example: *Cadder* v *HM Advocate* 2020 found that Scottish police were in breach not only of the ECHR but also of the Scotland Act 1998 in the way that they detained suspects.	The rule of law is what politicians say it is. Since the UK Constitution is not entrenched, parliaments, dominated by governments, can overturn rights and liberties with a simple act of Parliament.
It asserts common law rights. Example: in *Dover District Council* v *CPRE Kent* 2017, the court ruled that when planning permission has been granted against the advice of its own professionals, local authorities are obliged under common law to give their reasons for doing so.	Rights have better legal standing and greater legitimacy when confirmed by Parliament. Example: the Countryside and Rights of Way Act 2000 clarified and confirmed the common law 'right to roam' in the countryside.
The court rules on freedom of information cases. Example: in *Evans* v *Attorney General* 2015, the Supreme Court ruled that the press had the right to publish royal correspondence that was sent to government departments by Prince Charles.	The government has frequently sought to limit the scope of the Freedom of Information Act. Example: following the court decision on royal correspondence, the Freedom of Information Act was amended to exempt the royal family from the scope of the Act.

Now test yourself

TESTED ⬤

3 Give two ways the judiciary can be seen as independent from government.
4 Give two ways the judiciary is limited in its ability to be independent from government.
5 Complete the following table on the Supreme Court and rights by including suitable counter-arguments.

How the Supreme Court protects rights	Limits/counter-arguments
Use of incompatibility statements	
Interpreting the ECHR	
Rulings on Freedom of Information Act cases	

Answers online

Exam tip

In the 'Relations between branches' topic, you may be asked to compare one branch with another on a specific issue. Therefore, a question about the Supreme Court may ask you to compare how well it protects rights in comparison with Parliament.

Remember

Students often wrongly assume that the European Convention on Human Rights, which is also part of UK law through the Human Rights Act, is controlled by the EU but it has nothing to do with the EU. It is controlled by a different body called the Council of Europe and therefore still applies despite the UK's withdrawal from the EU.

The influence of the Supreme Court on the executive and Parliament

The Supreme Court and the rest of the judiciary have various ways of controlling the power of both the UK Parliament and the government. In doing so they are preventing abuses of power and asserting the rights of citizens against the state. The methods they use include the following:

+ The courts enforce the European Convention on Human Rights (ECHR) when interpreting executive actions and in cases of judicial review.
+ The courts cannot set aside a piece of parliamentary legislation, but they can declare that a law is incompatible with the ECHR, which puts pressure on government to amend the law accordingly.
+ Similarly, the courts impose common law, often when asserting the rights of citizens.
+ The courts impose the rule of law, ensuring that all citizens are treated equally. This usually occurs as a result of judicial review.
+ In cases of *ultra vires* the courts decide whether a public body has exceeded its legal powers. This is also the case when judges rule that the government has exceeded its constitutional powers.
+ Public inquiries by judges can be very persuasive in forcing government to take certain actions.

Table 8.4 shows how and why the Supreme Court and the judiciary come into conflict with government.

Table 8.4 Judiciary–government conflicts

Issue	Detail
Sentencing in criminal cases	The judges wish to have a free hand in determining sentences on a case-by-case basis. The government, which is responsible for law and order, insists it needs to impose minimum sentences for some crimes, such as possession of weapons.
Rights	The judges have a duty to preserve human rights, but these may hinder the government's attempts to maintain national security, notably over terrorism.
Freedom of expression	While the government seeks to control the spread of religious extremism, by prosecuting extreme preachers and so on, the judges have a duty to preserve freedom of expression.
Freedom of information	The government believes some information should be secret in the national interest, while judges view sympathetically appeals under the Freedom of Information Act.
Judicial review	Judges have become more open to hearing appeals by citizens against public bodies which may have acted unlawfully, beyond their powers, been negligent or discriminated against certain people. Government claims too many judicial reviews inhibit its ability to govern.

Ultra vires Literally means 'beyond the powers'. *Ultra vires* is declared by courts when a public body takes action that is not given to it in law.

Remember

It is sometimes assumed that the UK Supreme Court can overturn a parliamentary statute. This is not so. It can recommend the repeal or amendment of a statute but cannot compel the UK Parliament to comply with its recommendations as Parliament is sovereign and it alone can decide these issues.

Answers and quick quizzes at **www.hoddereducation.co.uk/myrevisionnotesdownloads**

Ultra vires and judicial review

The term *ultra vires* has the following meaning and implications:
+ It literally means 'beyond the powers'.
+ Its value is to prevent public bodies from acting unlawfully.
+ It is a common subject of judicial review.
+ Citizens and organisations may appeal against a decision by a public body on the grounds that it was acting outside the powers granted to it by law.
+ The remedy, if a case is proved, is often the cancellation of the decision and sometimes compensation.

Now test yourself
TESTED ⬤

6 Look at the following descriptions. What is being described in each case?

Description	What is being described
The legal principle involved when a public body is accused of acting beyond its statutory powers	
The principle that judges must not be influenced by government when considering legal cases	
The principle that judges should not display any obvious political allegiance	

Answers online

Revision activity
Revise and remember two court cases which illustrate the following:
1 how the Supreme Court protected human rights in the UK
2 when a senior court declared an action by government to be *ultra vires*
3 when a senior court ruled against some kind of discrimination operated by a public body

The power of the Supreme Court

Table 8.5 considers the debate about whether the Supreme Court has become too powerful.

Table 8.5 The debate regarding the power of the UK Supreme Court

The UK Supreme Court is too powerful	The UK Supreme Court is not too powerful
Judicial review gives judges too much influence over public policy and the democratic process. Example: the two Brexit-related judicial reviews in the Supreme Court contributed to the delay in Brexit, despite its approval by the public in the 2016 EU referendum.	The court must wait for a case to be brought before it — it has no power to initiate a judicial review. The number of applications for judicial review fell by 44% between 2015 and 2019, largely as a result of cuts to legal aid for such challenges.
The creation of the Supreme Court makes conflict more likely, leading to a more active and independent court. Example: disputes over immigration, terrorism, human rights and Brexit have increased in recent years.	Politicians often undermine the independence of the Supreme Court and the judiciary more widely. Example: successive governments have set minimum terms for criminal offences and sentencing guidelines for judges.
The Human Rights Act allows the UK Supreme Court to interpret the ECHR and issue incompatibility statements, which hinders the ability of government to fight terrorism and curb immigration. Example: in 2019 the Supreme Court found that the Home Office policy of detaining asylum seekers prior to their removal amounted to 'false imprisonment'.	The courts are simply ensuring that rights are protected. A powerful executive with a majority in Parliament determines the range and scope of rights. Example: the Justice and Security Act (2013) allowed 'closed material proceedings' or secret courts into the justice system, something the Supreme Court is powerless to stop.

125

My Revision Notes: Pearson Edexcel A-Level Politics: UK politics second edition

The influence and effectiveness of the UK Parliament

This should be revised in conjunction with material in Chapter 5.

Although the common belief is that the executive dominates Parliament in the UK, there are some circumstances where Parliament exercises control. Table 8.6 lists the ways in which Parliament can control the executive.

Table 8.6 How Parliament can control the executive

How Parliament can control the executive	Example/Explanation
Parliament has the power to dismiss a government in a vote of no confidence.	James Callaghan's Labour government lost a vote of no confidence in 1979, triggering a general election.
Parliament has the reserve power to veto government legislation.	Theresa May sustained the largest parliamentary defeat in history when her Brexit deal was rejected by a majority of 230 votes in 2019.
The House of Lords can delay legislation for a year.	Plans to reduce tax credits were blocked by the Lords in 2015.
The Commons can amend legislation.	After pressure from backbenchers, the government agreed to an amendment to the Internal Market Bill in 2020, removing the government's ability to override parts of the EU Withdrawal Agreement.
The House of Lords can also amend legislation, although its decisions can be reversed in the House of Commons.	The Lords backed the so-called Dubs amendment to the EU Withdrawal Agreement Bill in 2020, which aimed to protect the rights of child refugees after Brexit. This amendment was then rejected by the House of Commons.
The government may face a backbench rebellion.	The Conservative Party dropped plans to relax Sunday trading laws in England after 27 Tory backbenchers sided with the opposition in 2016.
The departmental select committees have become increasingly effective in calling government to account.	In December 2020 the Commons Culture, Media and Sport Select Committee criticised the government for a 'lack of effective planning' in rolling out gigabit-capable broadband.
When the government allows a free vote, MPs or peers may vote according to their beliefs rather than party allegiance.	David Cameron allowed Conservative MPs a free vote on legalising gay marriage.
Ministers are obliged to present themselves before Parliament to account for their decisions and policies.	The increase in the number of urgent questions has forced ministers to answer before Parliament at shorter notice and at more frequent intervals.

Executive dominance of the UK Parliament

There are a number of ways in which the executive can control Parliament and a number of structural weaknesses which Parliament has to accept. Executive dominance of Parliament has sometimes been described as an elective dictatorship. Table 8.7 lists the ways in which the executive can control Parliament.

> **Elective dictatorship**
> An expression used by Conservative politician Lord Hailsham in 1976; the belief that if the governing party enjoys a parliamentary majority, it is able to drive through any legislation it wishes.

Table 8.7 How the executive controls Parliament

How the executive can control Parliament	Example/Explanation
The government usually enjoys the support of the majority of MPs in the House of Commons. It can expect to win virtually every critical vote.	Boris Johnson's 80-seat Commons majority allowed his government to introduce a post-lockdown system of tiers for different parts of the country, despite misgivings from backbenchers.
The patronage of the prime minister demands the loyalty of most of their party's MPs. So too do the influence and sanctions of the whips.	The removal of the whip in September 2019 from 21 Conservative MPs who voted against the government on Brexit showcased how the prime minister can not only reward loyalty but also punish those who are disloyal.
The government controls the legislative process and can block most amendments from the floors of the Commons and Lords.	In 2020, the government overturned five House of Lords amendments to its Brexit bill before the EU Withdrawal Agreement Bill was passed into law.
The House of Lords can delay but cannot veto legislation.	The Parliament Act 1949 limits the Lords' power of delay to one year.
The Salisbury Convention means that the Lords cannot block legislation for which the government has an electoral mandate.	Any specific proposal contained in the winning party's manifesto ought not to be blocked by the House of Lords.

The changing relationship between Parliament and the executive

Making links

When mentioning the size of a government's majority, refer to the first-past-the-post electoral system.

Table 8.8 shows how the relationship between government and Parliament can change according to circumstances and depends upon a number of factors.

Table 8.8 The changing relationship between the UK Parliament and the executive

Factor	How this factor increases the influence of Parliament	How this factor retains executive influence
Type of government	A government without a majority in the House of Commons is more likely to suffer defeats in both chambers. Example: the House of Lords held up the reforms to the welfare system proposed by the coalition government between 2010 and 2015.	The government normally enjoys a Commons majority, allowing it to push through the legislation it wants. Example: Boris Johnson's 80-seat majority allowed for the smooth passing of the EU Withdrawal Act 2020.
Issue	Any issue that divides the governing party could result in greater parliamentary scrutiny. Example: Theresa May's government lost several votes on Brexit.	Some issues unify the governing party and divide the opposition. Example: the vote on military action against ISIS in 2015.
The authority of the prime minister	A weak prime minister will face far greater scrutiny in Parliament. Example: John Major's government barely survived a vote of no confidence.	A strong prime minister can often evade parliamentary scrutiny. Example: Tony Blair attended Parliament less frequently in his first term in office than any of his postwar predecessors.
The government's handling of emergencies and events	If a government is perceived to be failing or lacking decisiveness, parliamentary scrutiny will increase. Example: Tory backbench MPs rebelled over changes to the English tier system of controls to address Covid-19 in December 2020.	It is generally accepted that the government should have the flexibility to respond to emergencies. Example: the Coronavirus Act 2020 gave extensive powers to the government to slow the spread of the virus.

> **Remember**
>
> Remember that the relationship between Parliament and the executive is not a static model; it is constantly changing according to circumstances. The most important circumstances include the size of the government's majority and the strength and unity of both the governing and opposition parties.

The nature of the European Union

There are four main features of the European Union (EU):

+ It is a customs union. This means that there are no tariffs (import taxes) on any goods and services being traded between member states. It also means that member states cannot have separate trade agreements with countries outside the EU. All external trade agreements apply to all members.
+ It is a free, single market. This means there can be no barriers to the free movement of goods, services, finance, labour or people between member states. Citizens of a member state are also citizens of the European Union and can live wherever they wish within the Union and, broadly speaking, enjoy common citizenship rights.
+ It is a partial political union. There are laws made by the institutions of the European Union which apply throughout the Union. These laws ensure that all members compete on a level playing field using the same laws.
+ Some but not all member states are part of a monetary union. This means they use the same currency, the euro.

In addition, the EU was based upon the principle of four freedoms of the single market.

> **European Union (EU)** A political and economic group of European countries.
>
> **Four freedoms (of the EU)** The principle of freedom of people, of labour, of capital and of goods and services.

The political impact of the UK's decision to leave the European Union

+ In the 2016 EU referendum, 51.9% voted for the UK to leave the EU and 48.1% voted to remain.
+ Two prime ministers have been forced to resign over the issue — David Cameron immediately after the referendum and Theresa May after failing to win parliamentary support for her Brexit deal.
+ Both the governing party and the opposition became deeply divided over the next steps to take, which made it difficult to pass legislation relating to Brexit.
+ Some MPs called for a second referendum and others called for a soft Brexit.
+ Meanwhile, the pro-Brexit faction of the Conservative Party supported a 'clean break' or hard Brexit.
+ After the referendum, two subsequent general elections were called in 2017 and 2019, the latter of which restored a Commons majority to the Conservative Party with a mandate to 'get Brexit done'.
+ The EU Withdrawal Act was passed in January 2020, resulting in the UK leaving the EU's political institutions.
+ The EU and the UK agreed to a trade deal in December 2020, which was subsequently approved by Parliament. A different set of trading arrangements will exist for Northern Ireland.

> **Soft Brexit** The scenario where the UK would keep as close a relationship to the EU as possible, continuing to be a member of the customs union and single market.
>
> **Hard Brexit** The scenario where the UK would leave the customs union and single market and not be subject to EU rules or to decisions handed down by the European Court of Justice. The EU Withdrawal Act and subsequent trade deal with the EU could be considered to be a hard Brexit.

The constitutional impact of the UK leaving the European Union

The following changes will occur in relation to the UK Constitution:

+ The European Court of Justice will no longer have any jurisdiction in the UK and will cease to be the highest court of appeal on EU matters.
+ There may be an increasing divide between Scotland, which voted largely to remain in the EU referendum, and England, which voted to leave, resulting in further calls for Scottish independence.
+ Under the terms of the withdrawal agreement with the EU, Northern Ireland will continue to follow many of the EU's rules to avoid customs checks on the border it shares with the Republic of Ireland. Therefore, there is now a part of the UK that has a separate trading relationship with the EU.
+ The UK government and Parliament will, for many years potentially, become preoccupied with deciding whether current EU laws and regulations should be permanently transferred into UK law or scrapped.

Making links

When mentioning how different parts of the UK are having to follow EU rules (Northern Ireland) while others are not, refer to the democratic deficit, especially since Northern Irish MPs voted against this arrangement.

The changing location of sovereignty in the UK

There are many different forms of sovereignty, which are described in Table 8.9.

Table 8.9 Different forms of sovereignty

Form of sovereignty	Description
Legal sovereignty	This refers to formal power, which usually lies where laws are made. In the UK, Parliament is seen to have legal sovereignty.
Political sovereignty	This refers to the body, institution or group that *in practice* holds the most influence over decision making. In the UK, the governing party, the cabinet and the prime minister are often thought of as having political sovereignty, in part due to their dominance over Parliament.
Popular sovereignty	Popular sovereignty rests with the electorate, which votes in referendums and elections, the outcome of which are *in practice* binding on Parliament.
Devolved sovereignty	Parliament agrees for other bodies or institutions to take decisions. These 'devolved' powers can be taken back by the UK Parliament at a later date.

Legal sovereignty Where formal, legal power is supposed to reside.

Political sovereignty Those individuals, groups or institutions that exercise sovereignty in practice. It is the reality of where power resides.

The decision to leave the EU has heightened the debate about where sovereignty lies in the UK and whether Parliament in particular has 'won back' its legal sovereignty. Table 8.10 considers the debate about parliamentary sovereignty.

Table 8.10 Is Parliament still sovereign?

Parliament is sovereign	Parliament is not sovereign
Brexit has meant that the UK Parliament once again enjoys full legal sovereignty. Example: prior to Brexit, it was accepted in the **Factortame Case** that EU law had 'primacy' over UK law. The UK Parliament could not introduce a law that conflicted with EU law, but now it can.	Many of the powers returning to the UK will not be subject to parliamentary jurisdiction but instead be wielded by government ministers in the form of secondary legislation.
Political sovereignty is not fixed and is restricted by parliamentary assertion. A party with a thin or non-existent majority will find it much more difficult to control the parliamentary agenda. Example: in spring and autumn 2019, Parliament voted to take over the agenda of Parliament using **Standing Order 24**, wresting it away from government and allowing it to initiate its own votes on Brexit.	Political sovereignty rests with the governing party, the cabinet and the prime minister. The fusion of powers allows the government to sit in Parliament and to control the agenda. Example: despite Parliament's approval of the **Article 50** process, the decision to comply with requests to 'extend Article 50' and thus delay Brexit rested with the prime minister and cabinet.
If the popular will is divided, as shown by the EU referendum and also by the 2017 general election, the net effect is to empower ordinary MPs who hold more power in a hung parliament, thus allowing Parliament to take control of decision making.	Popular sovereignty has challenged parliamentary sovereignty. Example: the outcome of the EU referendum in 2016 served as an instruction to Parliament to deliver on Brexit.
Despite devolution, Parliament retains reserved powers, and still takes the major decisions affecting the nation. The **Sewel Convention** is not legally binding and so the devolved bodies can be ignored by Parliament. Example: the Supreme Court ruled in 2017 that the devolved bodies could not reject what Parliament passes in relation to Brexit.	Parliamentary sovereignty has been effectively devolved to newly created institutions such as the Scottish Parliament. Example: the Sewel Convention implies that the devolved bodies should be asked for their consent to laws passed by Parliament that are considered to be under the jurisdiction of the devolved administrations.

Factortame Case A ruling by the former Law Lords which asserted that EU laws on fishing rights took priority over a UK law that banned foreign vessels in UK waters.

Standing Order 24 A rule of the House of Commons that allows an MP to request an emergency debate on a particular topic. The Speaker can decide whether to accept or reject the request. Most often the request is refused, but the Speaker is more likely to be swayed if the government lacks a majority.

Article 50 The legal mechanism for a member of the EU to leave the EU. It is essentially a notice period that a country gives to leave, but this notice period can be extended by mutual consent.

Sewel Convention The expectation that the UK Parliament would not normally legislate in areas that are considered to be part of the jurisdiction of the devolved bodies.

Exam tip

To answer a question on parliamentary sovereignty, it is important to consider conflicting claims of where sovereignty lies. It is perhaps safe to argue that the UK has 'multiple sovereignties' in conflict with each other.

Now test yourself TESTED ⬤

10 Look at the types of sovereignty listed in the left column. Give examples to support the idea that they exist in the UK.

Description	When sovereign
Devolved sovereignty	
Popular sovereignty	
Political sovereignty	

Answers online

Making links

The shift in sovereignty from Parliament to the devolved bodies links to the adoption of a more pluralistic democracy, as it allows pressure groups more access points to exercise influence.

Exam practice

1 Evaluate the view that the executive can control the UK Parliament. [30]

2 Evaluate the view that, now the UK has left the EU, Parliament has become sovereign once again. [30]

3 Using the source, evaluate the view that the UK Supreme Court has too much power. [30]

The creation of the UK Supreme Court has served to increase the prestige and status of the judiciary and appears to have emboldened that body to take on the government. The geographical separation from Parliament has increased the top court's independence. Supreme Court judges can use the power of judicial review, whereby actions of government and other bodies can be declared 'ultra vires' (acting beyond powers given in law). The Human Rights Act has allowed the court to stretch its powers still further. It regularly compels ministers to release information they do not want to release. Critics believe that the court is now acting as an imperial judiciary. Its decisions surrounding Brexit further increased the suspicion that the court was sticking its nose in where it shouldn't.

Yet Parliament is ultimately sovereign and a government with a strong majority in the House of Commons can override court decisions. The current Conservative government, returned to office in December 2019 with a majority of 80 seats, may well review what the court can and cannot do. Far from being too powerful, the court is weak when compared to its US counterpart, which has an entrenched constitution to refer to, unlike judges in the UK where there are no higher constitutional laws. The court cannot be proactive and has no enforcement power. In a similar way to ministers, the Supreme Court cannot make rulings that defy laws made by Parliament. The Supreme Court cannot overturn statute law even if those laws go against the European Convention of Human Rights (ECHR).

Source: original material

In your response you must:
+ compare and contrast the different opinions in the source
+ examine and debate these views in a balanced way
+ analyse and evaluate only the information presented in the source

Answers and quick quiz 8 online

Exam skills

Exam questions typically focus on the power that one branch of government can wield against another. It is good practice to think of all the ways that the branches can do this and also how they might be limited. Below is a table that can be filled in to help you plan and revise for these sorts of questions. Go back over this chapter and add to this table every time you come across a power or a limit that one branch has against another. A few examples have been filled in for you.

Branch	Parliament is limited by...	Executive is limited by...	Judiciary is limited by...
Parliamentary power		Votes of no confidence	Parliamentary sovereignty
Executive power	Royal prerogative		Ignoring of incompatibility statements
Judicial power	Issuance of incompatibility statements	Judicial review	

Summary

You should now have an understanding of:
+ the role of the judiciary and the UK Supreme Court
+ Supreme Court judgments — you will need to be able to refer to several important ones
+ judicial neutrality and independence and whether they exist in reality
+ the Supreme Court and the protection of rights
+ the influence of the Supreme Court upon government and Parliament, specifically its power of judicial review
+ the debate about the power of the Supreme Court
+ how Parliament can control the executive
+ how the executive can control Parliament
+ the circumstances or factors that affect the relationship between Parliament and the executive
+ the features and principles (four freedoms) of the EU
+ the political and constitutional impact of the UK's decision to leave the EU
+ the different forms of sovereignty
+ the debate about whether Parliament is sovereign

Glossary

Term	Definition	Page(s)
Additional member system (AMS)	An electoral system used for a number of elections in the UK, including the Scottish and Welsh Parliamentary elections. AMS maintains elements of FPTP, specifically the use of constituencies.	45
Authoritative works	Historical books and documents that clarify the meaning of constitutional principles.	75
Backbenchers	MPs and peers who are not senior members of their party and so sit in Parliament behind the front bench.	92
Cabinet	A body of 20–25 senior ministers and other important senior party figures, such as the chief whip, whose meetings are chaired by the prime minister.	103
Class dealignment	A trend whereby fewer people associate themselves with belonging to a particular social class, decreasing the impact of class on voting behaviour.	57
Classical liberals	Liberals following a form of liberalism harking back to the nineteenth century which proposed the maximisation of personal freedom and the minimal state.	34
Coalition government	Where two or more parties are in power. While no party enjoys a majority of seats on their own, combining the seats of the parties in power gives them a majority of seats overall.	43
Codified constitution	A constitution that can be found in one single document and so has one single source. Constitutional laws are seen as superior to ordinary laws and have a separate amendment procedure.	72
Collective ministerial responsibility	The convention that ministers must support government decisions in public, regardless of any private reservations. If they are unable to do so, then they should resign.	107
Confidence and supply	An arrangement between the governing party and a smaller party in a hung parliament whereby the smaller party agrees to support the government in key votes, such as on the budget and on votes of no confidence. In return, the smaller party usually secures support on a specific policy.	98
Constitution	A set of rules that establishes a country's governmental and political system.	71
Conventions	Unwritten political rules or practices that are considered binding, such as the Salisbury Convention that prevents the House of Lords from blocking manifesto proposals.	75
Common law	Unwritten laws that have not been passed by Parliament but have passed down through history in the form of judicial precedents.	75
	Unwritten law that can be declared valid by a court on the grounds that certain rules have existed for a long time and are generally accepted by people as law. Common law often concerns the rights that citizens enjoy. Such law is passed down through judicial precedents.	
Democratic deficit	Where standards of a functioning democracy have fallen short, owing to the lack of certain features associated with democracy or due to barriers that prevent those democratic features from being effective.	13
Devolution	A process whereby power, but not legal sovereignty, is distributed away from central government to regional governments.	76
Direct democracy	A political system where the people themselves make political decisions. The modern equivalent is the use of referendums and initiatives within representative democracies.	10
Disillusion and apathy	Traits that force down levels of turnout. They may be the result of low esteem for the political class or a general lack of interest in politics and a suspicion that politics cannot change things for many people.	63

Elective dictatorship	An expression used by Conservative politician Lord Hailsham in 1976; the belief that if the governing party enjoys a parliamentary majority, it is able to drive through any legislation it wishes.	126
Entrenched constitution	A constitution that has special arrangements to safeguard it from being amended by a temporary government or legislature. Entrenchment is closely associated with codified constitutions.	72
European Union (EU)	A political and economic group of European countries.	128
Executive	Also known as 'the government', this is the collective name for the prime minister, cabinet, junior ministers, government departments and their staff.	103
First-past-the-post (FPTP)	The electoral system used in UK general elections; the candidate with the most votes in a constituency wins a seat in the House of Commons.	42
Four freedoms (of the EU)	The principle of freedom of people, of labour, of capital and of goods and services.	133
Franchise or suffrage	Both terms essentially mean the right to vote. In modern democracies suffrage is extended to all adults, with no groups excluded. A system which does exclude some or all citizens from voting cannot be described as democratic.	14
Fusion of powers	The government is made up of individuals who are members of either the House of Commons or the House of Lords.	74
Governing competency	A general feeling among voters that a party is either very competent in governing or much less competent. Competency refers largely to sound economic policies, sensible foreign policy and decisiveness in office.	60
Government department	A part of the executive with a specific responsibility over a policy area.	103
House of Commons	The elected and most powerful chamber of Parliament. Its membership consists of 650 MPs.	90
House of Lords	The unelected chamber of Parliament. Its main role is to examine and revise legislation from the House of Commons.	90
Hung parliament	Occurs when no party has a majority of seats; either a minority government or a coalition government is formed.	133
Individual ministerial responsibility	The principle that ministers are responsible for their personal conduct and for the work of their department.	105
Individual rights	Rights that belong to a person regardless of personal characteristics. They apply to all individuals regardless of race, religion or gender.	23
Insider groups	Pressure groups with access to decision makers, which means that their tactics tend to be more discreet and behind closed doors, relying upon a network of close links to advisors and politicians. Outsider groups do not usually have such close contact with decision makers and therefore need to resort to methods that seek public support and media attention.	18
Judiciary	A general term referring to the whole legal system. In terms of politics, the senior judiciary are those judges and courts that make decisions of wider political significance.	120
Judicial independence	The principle that the judiciary should be free of political interference and criticism, particularly from the executive.	133
Judicial neutrality	The principle that judges should not be influenced by their personal opinions and that they should remain outside of party politics.	121
Judicial review	The power to declare actions of government or other bodies such as local authorities as *ultra vires* or acting beyond their power given to them in law.	120
Left wing	Ideologies, ideas and policies that are associated with socialism, including redistribution of income, regulation of the excesses of capitalism, protection for workers' rights, a stress on state welfare and state control of some major industries.	29
Legal sovereignty	Where formal, legal power is supposed to reside.	129
Legislative bill	A proposal presented to Parliament for legislation. Once passed in Parliament, a bill becomes an Act of Parliament.	91

Legislative output	The number of bills that are enacted into law.	97
Legislative quality	Refers to a situation whereby bills have received appropriate scrutiny and have not been rushed through Parliament.	97
Legitimacy	A situation whereby the outcome of elections is accepted, and the authority of government is recognised by the public.	10
Lobbyists	Individuals or companies paid to persuade decision makers to favour a particular group or cause.	20
Neo-conservativism	Emphasises a belief in order and traditional values, and a wariness of immigration. Neo-conservatives primarily focus on the structure of society and the political system. They believe that society is naturally hierarchical.	30
New Labour	The centrist faction in the Labour Party that promotes equality of opportunity rather than absolute equality and that advocates a mixed economy. It is comfortable with private involvement in welfare provision.	32
Neo-liberalism	Places greater emphasis on limited government intervention in the economy. Free markets and privatisation are promoted while welfare is opposed due to the fear that it leads to dependency.	30
New Right	A faction within the Conservative Party that combines neo-conservative beliefs (traditional values and an emphasis on law and order) with neo-liberal beliefs (limited state intervention in the economy and low taxation).	30
Noblesse oblige	A French expression that essentially means that the rich have responsibility to the poor.	30
Majority government	One party is in power and enjoys a majority of seats in the House of Commons.	43
Mandate	The authority, granted by the people at elections, of the winning party at a general election. The newly elected government has the authority to carry out its election proposals contained in the party manifesto.	62
Manifesto	A set of commitments produced by each party at the start of an election campaign.	62
Marginal seat	A constituency where more than one party has a realistic chance of winning the seat at an election and the outcome of the election is likely to be close.	42
Minister	An MP or a peer who takes a position in government, usually in a specific government department.	104
Minority government	One party makes up the government, but it does not have a majority of seats. It often governs by making deals with other parties to support it on key votes, which is what the Conservatives did with the DUP between 2017 and 2019. Such deals are called 'confidence and supply' arrangements.	43
Modern liberals	Liberals who emerged after classical liberalism in the late nineteenth century. While still insisting on maximum freedom, they also accept that the state should intervene to create greater equality of opportunity, welfare and social justice. Modern liberals also support social diversity.	35
Old Labour	The faction of the Labour Party that supports traditional socialist principles. These include greater social equality, an active role for the state in the economy and generous welfare provision.	32
One Nation	A faction within the Conservative Party that is concerned with social cohesion. As a result, it is supportive of the welfare state and advocates a mixed economy rather than one that solely promotes privatisation.	30
Opposition	A general term referring to all parties that are not part of the government. 'Her Majesty's official opposition' refers to the second largest party in the House of Commons.	95
Parliament	A name given to the legislature in many countries. It has the dual role of legitimising proposed legislation and representing the people.	90
Parliamentary ping-pong	Occurs when the two houses cannot agree on the wording of a bill, which is then sent back and forth between the two chambers for amendments.	98

Answers and quick quizzes at **www.hoddereducation.co.uk/myrevisionnotesdownloads**

Parliamentary privilege	An ancient principle that protects MPs from external pressure and specifically means they cannot be prosecuted or sued for anything they may say in the House of Commons. It also implies that the monarch can never interfere with the work of the UK Parliament.	92
Parliamentary sovereignty	The concept that Parliament is the supreme decision-making body in the UK.	72
Participation crisis	A concern that fewer people are taking part in political activity, leading to a crisis in democratic legitimacy.	15
Partisan dealignment	A trend whereby fewer voters are committed to, or loyal to, a specific party.	57
Party system	A reference to how many parties achieve representation and have an influence on the politics of a country.	37
Patronage	The power of appointment and dismissal. In relation to the prime minister, patronage over ministerial offices gives them great power because it promotes loyalty among those who are promoted or who hope to be promoted.	108
Payroll vote	Senior ministers and junior ministers who, since they owe their promotion to the prime minister, can be relied upon to vote in favour of government legislation.	108
Personal mandate	The individual authority claimed by prime ministers to steer the policy direction of government, largely as a result of their popularity, recent election victories and personal attributes.	111
Plurality	A term used to describe 'the most votes'. If a candidate receives a plurality then they have won more votes than any other candidate. That does not mean that they have received an 'absolute majority', which is what happens when a candidate wins 50%+ of the vote. Under FPTP, a winning candidate only requires a plurality of the vote, not an absolute majority.	42
Pluralist democracy	A political system and/or society where there is widespread acceptance or 'tolerance' of different groups and lifestyles, where freedom of expression and association are respected, where many parties and pressure groups may operate and where there are independent media. The term also implies that power is dispersed and not concentrated.	13
Political sovereignty	Those individuals, groups or institutions that exercise sovereignty in practice. It is the reality of where power resides.	129
Presidential government	A system where the legislature and executive are separate from each other and where the leader is directly elected.	116
Prime ministerial government	Political circumstances in which the prime minister dominates policy making and the whole machinery of government.	112
Primus inter pares	A Latin term meaning 'first among equals'. It is applied to the prime minister, seen as the most important member of the cabinet but not one who is domineering.	112
Private members' bills	Legislation introduced by individual backbench MPs. These bills do not necessarily have the backing of government.	92
Proportional representation (PR)	A description of any electoral system that awards seats broadly in proportion to the votes cast for each party.	45
Public bill committees	Also referred to as legislative committees, these are temporary committees established to give line-by-line scrutiny of a specific bill and to propose amendments.	90
Referendum	An occasion when voters are asked to decide upon an issue of public importance.	10
Representative democracy	A political system where the citizens elect representatives who make decisions on their behalf and are accountable to them.	10
Right wing	Ideologies, ideas and policies that promote free market capitalism and acceptance of social and economic inequality, and that advocate a limited role for the state, including low taxation and welfare levels, the promotion of free markets and a hard line on crime.	29

135

Royal prerogative	The unwritten powers that have passed from the monarch to the prime minister. These include powers of patronage, acting as commander-in-chief and negotiating foreign treaties.	109
Rule of law	The principle that equal justice should apply to all. This by extension requires the government to follow the law as laid down by parliament.	73
Safe seat	A constituency where one party is so dominant that it is almost unthinkable that it will not win the seat at every election.	42
Salisbury Convention	A convention that ensures major government bills that are mentioned in an election manifesto will not be voted down by the House of Lords. It acknowledges that the unelected House of Lords lacks the legitimacy to block bills that a winning party pledged to introduce at the last general election.	95
Secondary legislation	Much of the business of government is conducted using secondary or delegated legislation. These are orders made by ministers which require relatively little parliamentary control. The power to make such orders is given to ministers in primary legislation.	105
Select committee	A permanent committee of backbench MPs that scrutinises the work of government departments.	90
Separation of powers	The powers of the different branches of government are clearly defined and separated, as are the personnel.	74
Sewel Convention	The expectation that the UK Parliament would not normally legislate in areas that are considered to be part of the jurisdiction of the devolved bodies.	130
Single transferable vote (STV)	A proportional electoral system that is used for Northern Irish Assembly elections and Scottish local elections. Constituencies are of a larger size than under FPTP and elect several representatives rather than just one. Voters rank candidates in order of preference. To get elected, a candidate must receive a set number of votes, known as a quota.	47
Social class	The classification of people based on their occupations and, to some extent, their income. Social class is often expressed using social grades AB, C1, C2 and DE, which divide the population up into different professions.	56
Statute law	Any law that has been passed by the UK Parliament and has received royal assent.	75
Supply days	Also known as opposition days, these are parliamentary days that are under the control of opposition parties rather than the government.	96
Supplementary vote (SV)	An electoral system used to elect the London mayor and one that attempts to ensure that the winning candidate receives as close to 50% of the vote as possible. Voters have two votes — a first and second preference.	44
Supreme Court	The highest court in the UK political system.	120
Tactical voting	When voters choose a candidate who might not have been their preferred choice in order to keep the candidate they least like from winning.	42
Think tank	A body of experts brought together to investigate and offer solutions to economic, social and political problems.	20
Treaties	Agreements with external bodies that bind the UK in some way.	75
Turnout	The percentage of the electorate that casts a vote.	63
Ultra vires	Literally means 'beyond the powers'. *Ultra vires* is declared by courts when a public body takes action that is not given to it in law.	124
Uncodified constitution	A constitution that is not contained in a single document and has a number of different sources.	72
Unentrenched constitution	A constitution that can be amended by an individual government or parliament.	72
Unitary constitution	A constitution which establishes that legal sovereignty resides in one location. Under a unitary constitution, power can be delegated to subsidiary bodies, but this power can be returned to the sovereign body.	73
Vote of no confidence	A motion that, if passed, will effectively dismiss the government and force an election. If a vote of no confidence is defeated, it implies that Parliament has confidence in the government of the day. Theresa May's administration survived a vote of no confidence in January 2019.	93

Answers and quick quizzes at **www.hoddereducation.co.uk/myrevisionnotesdownloads**